self-awareness
through group dynamics

self-awareness

through group dynamics

BY RICHARD REICHERT

Pflaum/Standard
38 WEST FIFTH ST. • DAYTON, OHIO • 45402

ISBN 0-8278-0022-3
10022/18.8M/S3M-6-973

TABLE OF CONTENTS

INTRODUCTION

While working with a group of high school students last year, I was particularly impressed by one girl. Attractive, intelligent, popular, she participated freely with her comments and observations. She read the required material and could refer to it accurately. In many ways she was a model student, one who makes teaching so enjoyable. She seemed to be "learning" everything I was attempting to get across.

However, based on past experience I was not satisfied with these signs of growth. I have come to realize that, while we can bring students to an intellectual understanding of a topic and can train them in the skills related to a discipline, there is another area of education which ultimately determines the effectiveness of teaching. It is the area of the student's already existing attitudes, habits, and values — the life-style through which skills and knowledge are filtered. Real education must touch that life-style and at least present the possibility for the student to change it.

In the case of this girl, genuine learning took place only when she had participated in a group experience. We had been studying prejudice, and up to that point she could define it and quote various authors on it. But the experience was the turning point. It provided her with a concrete and personal awareness of the extent to which prejudice influenced her life. Only then was the education process completed for her.

Most teachers are becoming aware of this aspect of education, the need to relate a topic to the student's real-life attitudes. Though a subject like history or biology deals primarily with facts, these facts are intended to prepare a person to live a full, rewarding and productive life. If these facts are received by a person already pre-conditioned by a selfish or anti-social life-style, the facts alone will do little to enrich his living. Just including a unit on certain values or social attitudes is not sufficient. For when you are dealing with such matters you are involved with a gestalt of feelings, prejudices, emotions, patterns of reaction. You just don't teach (or un-teach) attitudes in the same way you teach skills or facts. You are involved in an entirely different methodology. It must be psychological rather than intellectual.

It is with such a methodology that this book is concerned. The goal is to affect the life-style of the student. The sessions employ the same principles of group dynamics which are being found so effective by industry in areas like management training, by social workers in the area of community relations and even by therapists in rehabilitation clinics. They aim at affecting the life-style of the person involved and not just imparting knowledge.

These, briefly, are the principles of this kind of methodology:

1. Because a student develops a life-style through series of life experiences and through a multitude of relationships over a period of time, he often has arrived at attitudes and habits without being aware of them. The first step in influencing a life-style is to make the student conscious of his own. Once this is achieved, he can either reject it or actively reinforce it.

2. To bring the student to an awareness of his life-style, you must create a situation in which he will react in his "typical" way. For example, he may regard himself as a very trusting person, or he may never really have been concerned about

whether or not he is a trusting person. By creating a situation in which his ability to trust others will be tested, he can discover, with the teacher's help, just what role trust is actually playing in his life and in his relation with others.

3. Other persons greatly influence the kind of life-style we adopt. Also we depend very much on others to truly know and understand ourselves. For these reasons, any education regarding life-style should be experienced in a group setting where free interaction takes place. This interaction is an essential element in a person's discovery and judgment of his life-style.

In short, the methodology developed throughout this book is intended to bring a student to an *awareness* of his own life-style and the options he has by creating a *group situation* in which he can *react in his "typical" way* to a particular value or relationship.

One point should be made clear. In this methodology there is no question of group pressure, manipulation, or force which would rob a person of his freedom to choose and preserve his own life-style. The aim is to make the student aware of his life-style and the options he has in developing it. While the teacher will possess strong convictions on most of the topics presented in the book, the methodology is not intended to allow the teacher to impose these convictions on the student. The individual's freedom is maintained.

To put all this another way, the object of this methodology is to develop insight — into oneself, others, and the basic values in human life. Insight (as opposed to information) implies decision and action. That is, a change or a reinforcement of one's life-style. Insight arranges a person's information into a meaningful pattern and evokes decisions which will call upon a person's skills. Insight should be the end product of education. Information and skills are valuable only in relation to insight.

This method is valuable any time a teacher wishes to lead his students to insight, regardless of the subject he teaches. It is easily adapted to the formal classroom situation or to the informal setting of many religious education programs. It can be used in coeducational situations or in groups of one sex. The topics suggested in the text can be used in their entirety in courses like psychology, sociology, and religion. Individual topics can be introduced separately according to the needs of a teacher. For example, a history teacher may wish to have a class on *Hawk and Dove*, or another on *Freedom and Responsibility* as these topics relate to the particular period of history he is covering. Even if the exercises have no immediate relation to the topic under consideration a teacher can use them as enrichment experiences, perhaps interjecting one each week. This could serve as a change of pace, and as an occasion for the teacher and students to know themselves and each other better. And since the topics covered in this text are not exhaustive, a teacher can develop topics on his own, using the basic principles of the methodology as his guideline.

Finally, this method has a limitation. It is intended to be supportive of an overall philosophy of education, not a substitute for one. That is, the overall educational environment must be concerned for human values and must be promoting them in various ways. This method can compliment such an environment. It can't work miracles on its own power.

General Instructions

I. When and with whom to use these exercises:

My own teaching experience indicates that these exercises can best be used in two situations.

A. As an introduction to a subject or a unit. In this situation the object is to lead the student to a deeper insight into a certain human value or human problem before you cover the course work, so he will gain more when he actually undertakes the material. For example, a sociology teacher about to introduce a unit on prejudice in society might begin with the exercise on *Prejudice* as kind of "test" so the class can see if or to what extent they are prejudiced. Based on their experience from the exercise, the students will then be better prepared to enter into and relate to themselves the information on prejudice covered in the unit. Or, a teacher in creative writing may wish to begin his course with the exercises on *Awareness* and *Creativity* to stimulate the students to approach the course more conscientiously.

B. When a human value or problem spontaneously arises out of the subject matter. In this situation the course is presented in the usual fashion, but when the students begin to question or become involved in a value or a problem, the exercise is introduced as a kind of "side track" to allow them to explore the value more deeply. For example, in a history course covering the Renaissance, the question of creativity will naturally arise. "Why did this period seem to produce so many creative geniuses?" From this comes the question, "Just what is creativity?" At that point the teacher could introduce the exercise on *Creativity*.

In both instances, the point is the same. The best time to introduce an exercise is when it can be related to the subject under consideration. In this instance the exercises are supplementary and used selectively.

Another occasion for using the topics is as a complete course in themselves. This can be done easily in religion programs or similar courses on human behavior. In these situations the exercises are an end in themselves and not a supplement.

The exercises in this book are intended primarily for 11th and 12th grade students. That is the age when students are psychologically drawn to explore deeper meanings and to re-examine childhood values. This does not mean that the exercises cannot be used with 9th and 10th grade students. It is doubtful, however, that the younger students are capable of the kinds of

13

insight the suggested topics intend to evoke. Usually they are not psychologically ready for in-depth discussion of these values since they are too self-conscious. But, the *methodology* can be applied successfully to topics more suited to younger students.

II. How to prepare for and introduce an exercise:

In terms of material preparation the main concern is just that — preparing the necessary materials and props ahead of time so the exercise goes smoothly and is not interrupted while someone is sent to find a stapler or a piece of paper. In terms of preparing the students mentally and introducing an exercise there are several suggestions:

A. The element of discovery, experimentation, testing a concept, should be stressed. Curiosity is one of man's strongest motivations and one thing man is most curious about is himself. So the exercises should be introduced as an activity which will tell us something about ourselves and others.

B. On the other hand, this element should not be over-stressed in such a way that the students become threatened and defensive. They must see the exercises as "non-judgmental," that is, the exercises are not intended to expose anyone's weaknesses or hidden faults. They are meant to explore human nature and human motivation in general, not someone's *private* personality. Thus the element of game or harmless contest should be pointed out.

C. Avoid any hint that you are tricking them into exposing their weaknesses to you or others. The best way to insure this is to make it clear that you yourself will participate in those exercises where you are not needed exclusively to conduct the exercise. You should "take your turn" along with the others in those activities where it is possible to do so.

D. On the practical level, stress that the exercises are not effective if the students do not follow the instructions seriously. For example, if an exercise calls for silence, it usually won't be

14

effective if there is an undercurrent of wise-cracks and laughter. So it is important that the students understand the instructions and are "settled" before you begin.

E.   Finally, explain to the students that they should try as much as possible to observe their feelings and reactions as they participate in a particular exercise, since these will play an important part in the discussion that follows. These feelings may range from embarrassment to anger, but every feeling is important.

III.   Getting the most out of the discussion:

The discussion portion of each session should flow from the immediate experience of the exercise. It is intended to lead the students to make generalizations about the value or problem being studied and to allow them to make practical application of these principles in their own lives. In order to achieve this purpose, several suggestions may be helpful:

A.   The teacher should keep in mind that these exercises cannot "fail"; they always provide a common experience to which the students can immediately react. While you hope the students will experience a particular emotion, they may just feel "stupid" or "embarrassed." If the students are made aware that *every* reaction is a valid one, that there is no *right* reaction, that *their* reaction is just as good as anyone else's, they will be willing to share it with others. The point is: discussion should always begin with the students' immediate reactions and feelings regarding the exercise. For example, the exercise on *The Clash of Individual Freedoms* is intended to evoke feelings of conflict and an awareness of the difficulty groups experience in coming to agreement on important matters. Some students may simply feel the exercise is "silly." They should be encouraged to give their honest reaction. But you should then follow up with questions such as: "Why did you think it silly?" "Why do you think the exercise didn't reflect 'how it really is'?" "How do you think it 'really is'?" "What do you think is the real problem concerning freedom?"

In short, any reaction can become the basis for serious discussion, provided you do not demand a particular reaction and provided you draw the students to make comments regarding their own attitudes about the topic.

B. When an exercise has been particularly successful and the students become very involved in the experience, you should be in no hurry to move into more general principles. You should encourage the students to "stay with the experience" as long as possible. Usually they themselves will begin to make more general observations in due time. Even if they do not, you now have a common experience to refer back to the next day or the next week when you wish to make your own observations about a particular value or problem.

For example, suppose you use the exercise on *Awareness* and the students become very involved with the immediate experience of their ability or inability to be aware of their surroundings. If they never move beyond this immediate reaction, you still will have the opportunity to refer back to the exercise in the next class as a starting point for a discussion about awareness in general and the role it should play in our lives. For the idea of awareness is no longer an abstraction for them. They *know what you mean* by the term and are now able to relate it to life in more general ways.

C. The questions provided with each exercise should be regarded as sample questions. Each teacher can choose from among them or develop his own along the lines he wishes to direct the discussion. The main point to remember, as experienced teachers know, is to prepare ahead of time the *kinds* of questions you want to ask, based on the kinds of ideas you want the students to examine. Such preparation does not mean a rote questioning which lacks spontaneity and gives students the impression that you are setting them up or that you have already decided what you expect them to say next. Your questions should reflect an honest inquiry into the reactions the students had to the exercise.

D. The notes which precede each exercise are meant, obviously, for the teacher. How you use them is up to you. The best way, it seems, would be to interject into the discussion those ideas from the notes which most impressed you — adding, perhaps, your own experiences of the topic under consideration. Or you may want to use these ideas as a basis for a lecture on the topic if you feel the class would be receptive to such an approach. But whatever form your teacher-input takes, it should emerge as ancillary to what the students are discussing. Nothing kills spontaneity more quickly than the realization by the students that the teacher is just letting them "talk," and then will present his prepared material regardless of what emerged in the student discussion.

E. Finally, if your class size is too large for all the students to participate in a discussion with you as discussion leader, divide the students into smaller groups and give each group a list of suggested questions. Or you may wish to verbally formulate a few questions for them. You can then circulate from group to group and by way of summary call upon each group to give short statements regarding the kinds of reactions they had to the questions. This allows each small group to compare its ideas with those of the other groups. However, do not introduce *your* list of questions until the students have had a chance to voice their immediate reactions. As pointed out above, discussion should flow from these reactions if it is going to avoid the danger of being irrelevant or too abstract.

IV. Some common mistakes to be avoided:

Based on past experience, I have discovered some mistakes that are often made regarding this kind of methodology. The following suggestions may help in avoiding them:

A. The exercises usually lose some of their effectiveness if they are used on the spur of the moment without proper preparation, or as a "filler" class which doesn't have any direct relation to the material you are covering in the course.

B. There is a temptation to over-explain the nature and purpose of an exercise. This often destroys the element of discovery and pre-programs students to give pat responses which they think you want them to make.

C. As mentioned earlier, don't be in too big a hurry to get into the theoretical principles you may want to expose to the students. These principles have the most lasting effect when they emerge naturally from reaction and discussion; that is, when they are seen as integral to the situation.

D. The suggested exercises are samples of a particular methodology. Feel free to adapt them as you see fit. If followed slavishly they can become forced and ineffective.

E. While every exercise suggested has been used successfully, don't expect every exercise to work equally well. In this kind of approach as elsewhere, you will have good days and bad days.

AWARENESS

Definition of Awareness

By the term "awareness" we are referring primarily to sensory awareness. The goal of this topic is to increase in students their sensory awareness of their surroundings.

There are several other levels to this topic, however, which should be kept in mind by the teacher as more long-range goals. There is the level of emotional awareness, sensitivity to one's own feelings and those of others. While sensory awareness is directed primarily at things, it provides a foundation for developing awareness of persons. Also, there is a kind of spiritual awareness, which might best be described as open-mindedness. It is the capacity to hold oneself open to "life" in the broadest and deepest sense of that word, to allow oneself to be touched by the goodness, beauty and meaning that is contained in human existence.

Perhaps an example of each kind of awareness will help. A person has sensory awareness when he is alive to sights, sounds, textures and smells that fill his daily life. Breakfast can be a sensory adventure – the smell of coffee and bacon, the sight of warm sunlight coming in the window, the feel of a soft table-cloth, the sound of morning birds. Yet for most of us, breakfast is a routine as dull as doing the dishes afterwards. A person is emotionally aware if he recognizes in himself feelings of anger when talking to a friend, even though his voice is low and his words are polite. A person is emotionally aware, or sensitive, when he can cut through a person's "I feel great" and recognize that the person actually feels very lonely, frightened or embarrassed. A person is spiritually aware or open-minded when he can discover dignity and goodness in an unshaven alcoholic asking him for a handout, or when he can listen — and hear — someone present religious or political views quite different from his own without being angered or threatened.

This topic aims only at developing in students an insight into the value of sensory awareness. It provides the foundation for the deeper kinds of awareness we just described.

Importance of Sensory Awareness

Sensory awareness is a basic part of being human. That is the main reason its nature and purpose deserves a place in any well-rounded education program.

The value of sensory awareness can best be seen by observing those who seem to possess it as a special gift: artists, musicians, poets. One of the sources for the creativity of these persons is their capacity to experience everyday things and events in a more intense way than others. It's as if their senses were greedy, constantly drinking in the slighest stimulus and draining it of its full import. For example, an artist can become ecstatic (literally outside himself) when he discovers a lowly marigold tucked away behind some log. Most of us — even if we had the sensory awareness to notice the marigold — would be satisfied with a brief glance. But each of us has far more capacity to receive sense stimuli than we realize. It is simply a question of cultivating the habit of awareness.

The result of a well cultivated sensory awareness is threefold: 1. Daily life is more exciting, since sensory awareness can make the most routine tasks and situations opportunities for new discoveries. 2. Sensory awareness develops both creativity and curiosity, the two qualities needed to be intellectually "alive." 3. Sensory awareness is the foundation for sensitivity to others and for spiritual sensitivity.

Contemporary society is now in the process of rediscovering the value of sensory awareness, a reaction to the dulling impact of our technological culture. This at least partially explains the popularity of Yoga, much of which is based on sensory awareness. Sensitivity institutes like Esalen in California have developed many programs aimed at developing sensory and emotional awareness. The popularity of William Shutz's little book *Joy*, and Rachel Carson's *A Sense of Wonder*, are other indicators of our society's concern for regaining its sensory awareness. Psychologists point out that the bold designs and bright colors of contemporary clothing are a reaction to a technological environment that is devoid of sensory excitement. And, as we'll see in a moment, the drug epidemic among youth can be traced at least partially to their attempt to fill the void created when sensory awareness is dulled.

Problems Related to Sensory Awareness
We face two kinds of problems in trying to introduce students to a deeper appreciation of sensory awareness. On the one hand, our technological society values efficiency and pragmatism, virtues to which children are introduced quite early in life. Taking time to notice little things in one's life seems either a waste of time or undisciplined day-dreaming. Schedules don't allow the luxury of concentrating on the softness of a chair, the patterns of light and shadow created by a table lamp, the sounds of a busy street. People who can get excited about such little things are often thought of in our society as odd – and the last thing a high school student wants is to be considered odd by his peers. Boys especially can feel uncomfortable about

this kind of awareness because too often it is considered a feminine trait. Socially, it is more acceptable for women to have a knack for noticing colors, remembering the arrangement of a room, observing the quality of a vase. This, however, does not mean such awareness cannot or should not be developed by men. But it may be difficult to convince a member of the football varsity of the desirability of this trait.

A second problem is that students eager for sensory experience now have available several artificial ways of "turning on," namely drugs like LSD, technological devices like psychedelic light shows and the hypnotic tempo of acid rock music and its variants. A person on an LSD trip can, for example, spend several hours gazing at the "whatness" of a rose. Or a person can go into a kind of trance while experiencing a light and rock music show. These things produce a kind of awareness which is akin to the sensory awareness we are talking about. But instead of expanding a person's capacity for sense experience they limit it to those artificially induced experiences, since every other experience seems pale by comparison. In this regard it is interesting to note that some drug rehabilitation centers use a kind of therapy aimed at developing normal sensory awareness as a substitute for drugs. And it works.

The point is that some students may not easily be convinced that sensory awareness is valuable. They may be so conditioned by the sterile, mechanical routine of modern life that they are out of touch with true sensation. Or they may be so jaded by artificially induced sensations that ordinary sensations have little effect on them. The teacher must keep this in mind and challenge the students to examine for themselves the kind of sensory life they are experiencing.

Cultivating Sensory Awareness
As in cultivating any habit, the key is motivation. A person

24

must see that sensory awareness is a human value, that he is missing out on a great deal of living because he has not cultivated his sensory perception. From that point on it is simply a question of periodically taking time to look, listen, feel, smell, taste. For example, it is a good exercise for a person to take a walk through his home, room by room, and attempt to notice everything he can: the color of the walls, the curtains, the pictures on the wall, the fixtures, lamps and other decorations, the arrangement of furniture, the lights and shadows, the odors. Or the same kind of thing can be done by pausing wherever you happen to be and trying to count the number of different sounds you can detect in that place. Or open the cupboard and take a sniff of the various foods and spices stored there. This type of thing can be expanded to include persons: the color of eyes, the shape of hands, the texture of hair, the uniqueness of each person's face.

In brief, a person cultivates sensory awareness by pausing at any place and time in his daily routine and attempting to focus his senses on as much of his surroundings as he can. He may want to feel things: rugs, furniture, tree bark, sidewalks, a flower. Or count the colors he can see around him. Or the sounds he can hear or the odors he can detect. Any place, any time, any sense is the right place, time and sense to begin cultivating sensory awareness. If a person would do this just once each day for one week, he would discover that his life begins to be filled with much more meaning and enjoyment. From there it is a short step to begin taking the same notice of other persons. Before long, a whole new inner universe of feelings and emotions will begin to unfold before him.

Suggested Exercise for Experiencing Sensory Awareness
Purpose:
    To illustrate in an experiential way that most of us are not

nearly as aware of our surroundings as we think, and thus to stimulate a discussion on the value of sensory awareness and the ways of cultivating it.

Preparation:

blindfolds

a six inch square piece of paper cut from an ordinary brown grocery bag

a small container of mustard

Instructions:

1. If you are working with a small group (six to ten) ask each person to put on a blindfold. If you have a larger group ask for six or eight volunteers (half boys and half girls in a mixed class).

2. After the blindfolds are on, instruct the students that you are going to ask them a series of questions. You will ask each in turn to attempt to answer the question. If their answer is a guess, they should indicate this. If they don't know the answer, they should so indicate. (Those observing may participate by closing their eyes, but they should not give "answers".) One person should keep a record of each person's answers. These are the questions:

   a. Ask the students to tell you what color the walls of the room are painted. (Or pick out some other dominant item like drapes, the bulletin board, etc.)

   b. Ask the students to tell you the color of *your* eyes.

   c. Ask them to tell if____(some popular boy in the class) is wearing a belt.

   d. Ask them to feel the piece of paper you prepared and tell them they have probably felt this kind of paper within the last several days. Can they say what kind of paper it is or where they felt it?

e. Ask them to try to identify the odor you present to them. (Hold the open mustard jar so each can smell it.)

You may expand this list of questions or substitute other similar items for the ones suggested above.

3. After you finish the questioning, the students may remove their blindfolds and you can present them with their "scores." As such these are meaningless, but you may wish to comment on them. For example, only two may have known the color of your eyes. while everyone recognized the odor of mustard, etc.

4. Now invite all the students (if some were just observers) to join in the second phase of the exercise. Explain that they are to try to observe as many things as they can in the room: colors, objects, persons, etc., within a set time limit — about two minutes. When the two minutes are up, ask everyone to be seated and to close his eyes. *It is important that they cooperate by keeping their eyes closed.* Now ask them specific questions about the room or about individual students. If a student thinks he can answer, he should raise his hand. If he gives the right answer, ask another question of the group. If he does not give the correct answer, ask another volunteer to try. Continue this for a few minutes or until the students get some feel of how observant or non-observant they are. Sample questions would be:

a. What kind of shoes is _____ wearing?
b. How many pictures are on the walls?
c. What is the color of _____'s shirt?
d. Where are the electrical outlets located? The heating outlets?
e. What color is the floor? The ceiling?

27

Discussion of Awareness

You can now introduce the discussion. Keep it moving by asking some of the following questions:

1. Why do you think we did this demonstration? What do you think I was trying to show?
2. Did you feel embarrassed or frustrated when you realized you couldn't answer some questions? How did you feel?
3. Why don't we tend to notice things like the color of people's eyes? Do you really feel it makes any difference? What things are we most likely to notice about others?
4. Do you think that most people are aware of how a paper bag feels, or if someone is wearing a belt? Would it make much difference if they did? What kind of difference?
5. Are you aware of what's in your home — the colors, the odors, the sounds, the feel of things, the people? Do you know the color of your mom's eyes? Your dad's, your brothers or sisters? Is it really important?
6. Can you name some things that most people never notice about you that you think it would be good for them to notice?
7. How do you feel when someone takes notice of what you are wearing, how you are feeling, the things you say? Why?
8. Why do artists and musicians and people like that tend to notice all kinds of little things that others overlook? What effect does it have on them?
9. Is this kind of habit of noticing little things possible in a society like ours? Is it necessary? Does it have any relation to how we treat each other?
10. If you wanted to develop an ability to be more aware of the little things in life, what are some ways you could do it?

Finally, you may want to summarize the discussion by clarifying points that were not fully developed or that did not come up in the student reaction.

CREATIVITY

Definition of Creativity

It is easier to describe creativity than it is to define it, its exact origins and nature being still a much debated topic among psychologists. So we will simply describe it: creativity is a capacity to see new relationships and possibilities in familiar objects, ideas or situations. For example, we would say a woman is creative if she can walk through a junk store, spy some battered old piece of furniture and see in it the possibilities — with the proper application of saw, sandpaper and paint — for a unique coffee table. A creative person, James Thurber for example, will take an everyday situation like a family dog chasing a cat and turn it into a hilarious adventure. Mankind's collective creativity is seen in what we have done with a simple concept like a wheel.

Creativity, then, is essentially the capacity to see new relationships. When these relationships involve mechanical things we usually say a person is inventive. When they involve concepts we call such a person intelligent. When they involve a bad situation which a person turns into new opportunities we say he is resourceful. When they deal with music, poetry or the fine arts, we say a person is creative. It is important to realize that creativity is not limited to the arts. Creativity is a way of life, not a special talent in the fine arts. Creativity can embrace every aspect of life, from our interpersonal relationships to the way we dispose of our garbage. For that reason, the topic can be profitably introduced into any academic subject.

This capacity to see new relationships is possessed in varying degrees by different people, and each person seems to have some kind of upper limit to his creativity. Or creativity might be restricted to only one aspect of life. For example a person may be very creative in terms of mathematical concepts but have very little creative capacity in verbal expression. Those who seem to have unlimited creativity in a particular field, such as Einstein in math, or those who seem to be creative in just about every aspect of life, such as Leonardo da Vinci, we call geniuses. The important point is that everyone has some creative capacity and this capacity can be developed. To develop it is to live more fully, to become more alive.

Importance of Creativity

It is well known that creative people are sought after in fields like engineering, advertising, management, marketing techniques, architecture. In the fine arts, creativity is the difference between success and failure. Too often we forget how valuable creativity is in daily life. In our modern, faceless, urban society of Social Security numbers and eleven digit telephone numbers creativity can mean the difference between mental health and neurosis. A person needs to be creative to survive today — "survive" in the sense of being self-directed, in possession of one's self, conscious. Routine, insignificant tasks, the sheer impact of one's littleness in society at large has a numbing, destructive effect on a person's self-awareness and self-direction. Certainly this experience — or the fear of it — is behind much of youth's rebellion against the establishment today. Unfortunately the rebellion itself lacks creativity in many instances. It becomes blind rage or bizarre individualism or simply "dropping out." It is the result of frustration rather than creativity.

Creativity, when applied to living rather than to specific tasks like engineering, epitomizes all of man's finest qualities. It rests upon sensitivity and awareness. It is triggered by intelligence. It is turned into action by freedom and courage. It is brought to fruition by patience and perseverance. It produces positive results, not destructive ones. To live creatively is to be all these things. And creativity can be developed.

Problems Related to Creativity

A teacher who wishes to pursue the topic of creativity with his students must keep in mind several problems. First, creativity is too often viewed only in terms of the fine arts, and students may regard it as "weird." Certainly, to bring up the topic of creativity to a bull-chested young athlete interested in auto mechanics involves the risk of turning him off completely. So it is important that you disabuse students of the narrow concept of creativity. Synonyms like resourcefulness, inventiveness, wit, adventuresomeness, as well as appropriate examples from various walks of life, can help broaden the student's concept of what you mean by creativity.

A more difficult problem with the topic of creativity lies in the fact that creative persons are often hard to deal with in a group situation where some conformity is required — the classroom, for example. For this reason, a teacher (or anyone responsible for getting a job done and maintaining order) is sometimes unwittingly threatened by the naturally creative person. His actions are interpreted as disobedience, lack of respect, negligence in following instructions, carelessness with prescribed details. As most teachers have experienced, the creative student is often bored by the classroom routine and becomes a discipline problem or an underachiever. For all these reasons, it is important that the teacher think through *his own* feelings about creativity before he begins presenting the topic to his class. And he must be willing to accept the consequences of cultivating this capacity. A roomful of creative students is never as neat and orderly as a roomful of conformists — but it is more exciting.

Finally, it is good to keep in mind that the student's creative capacity has probably been dulled to some degree by his experience in society: the home, the school, the church, government. These institutions usually praise order and discipline, reward the young child for conformity and punish him for his creative excursions. Certain inhibitions will have to be overcome before the student can begin to develop his creativity. While he may be able to see very quickly the value of creativity in relation to a particular profession, such as advertising, he may not be able to make the transfer to life in general. In other words, merely introducing the topic of creativity will not develop the student's capacity. It will have to be reinforced by the teacher, applied widely to various life situations, illustrated often as it occurs in others, and rewarded when practiced by the student. Because creativity is a way of life and not an academic subject, it is learned only through living. So the teacher's role is limited — but invaluable.

Cultivating Creativity

Creativity has its foundation in sensitivity and awareness, a topic discussed in the first chapter. Obviously a person will not discover new relationships if he is unaware of the present ones. So the first step in developing creativity is to develop a person's awareness of his surroundings.

The next step is to develop the habit of asking the question: What new possibilities are contained in this situation? Note, this is a different question than the "Why?" which we often encourage students to ask. "Why?" is a good question and could be creative, but it is only half a question. In the mouths of many students it is often more a challenge than an inquiry. Students ask it easily out of their natural inclination during adolescence to challenge all that adults present to them. "Why?" as students usually ask it in our classrooms, has a negative ring. It does not seek alternatives. It is often an attempt to find fault with existing ideas, traditions or practices.

The creative question, on the other hand, is rooted in the past and the present. It accepts these as given. And then it jumps into the future by focusing on *new possibilities* that can be created out of the given. Creativity is akin to an evolutionary leap, rooted in the past, but clearly new. Contrary to popular opinion, the creative person experiences and respects continuity in life. He is not a revolutionary trying to create something out of nothing (or out of the ashes of what he has destroyed). He creates new things out of what already exists. Authentic creativity demands order, albeit, an order that superficially appears to be disorder. That is why creativity rests upon the question: What new possibilities are contained in *this* situation?

In cultivating this capacity, the biggest single inhibiting factor is fear of failure or the ridicule that stems from failure. This is especially true in the adolescent who is very self-conscious and unsure of his true worth as a person. The last thing he needs is failure. For that reason creativity requires an atmosphere of acceptance, an environment where the only failure is "not to try." Creativity can best be cultivated, then, in game situations where nothing important is at stake except the fun of playing a game. In such instances every attempt at creativity is a success, even if it has no real practical value.

It is necessary to transfer a person's capacity for creativity from the theoretical level of the classroom into life situations. This is best done by problem-solving, using real problems the students face (for example, raising money for the school prom).

Once students are guided to approaching problems creatively, the step to living creatively is a relatively short one.

Finally, because people vary in their creative capacity, the less gifted can easily be discouraged if left to themselves. For such persons, group activities are the best situation for developing their self-respect and their creative potential. If each individual in a class is given a creative project, the less gifted will naturally compare his results with the more gifted and will doubt his own capacity. If a group is given a project, the less gifted will be able to contribute to the overall success, and will be able to do so at his own pace. Furthermore, he will be able to identify with the group's success, thus encouraging his own later efforts at creativity. For this reason, in classes of varying talents, group activities are the best way to introduce and cultivate creative capacities.

To sum up, cultivating the creative capacity involves five elements:

1. Developing sensitivity and awareness of one's surroundings.
2. Developing the habit of asking the creative question: "What new possibilities are contained in this situation?"
3. Providing a safe atmosphere for experimenting, where failure is eliminated.
4. Transferring creativity from theory to life by means of problem-solving.
5. Providing group situations for enhancing the creativity of the less gifted.

The exercise suggested here cannot do all of these things. It's intended primarily to aid the teacher in introducing the overall topic of creativity to the students. Once their interest is stimulated and they have some understanding of the topic, the teacher can develop their creative capacity through the various situations which arise out of the ordinary classroom situation.

Suggested Exercise for Experiencing Creativity
Purpose:
> To challenge the students to be creative in a specific task, thereby illustrating the creative capacity they possess, and to stimulate them to discuss in depth the role of creativity in their lives.

Preparation:
> wooden matches or tooth picks
> paper clips
> small pieces (6" x 6") of cardboard or posterboard
> rubber bands
> pencils
> scissors

Instructions:
1. For best results divide students into groups of four. If groups are larger, individual participation is lessened. In working with mixed groups, it is best to form groups of all boys and all girls for this exercise. Give each group a set of items composed of:
   1. four wooden matches or toothpicks
   2. one paper clip
   3. two rubber bands
   4. a small piece of cardboard

   Scissors and pencils can be made available for common use by the groups.
2. Instruct the groups that with the material you have presented they are to make some item that would be useful in any household kitchen. They are limited to the supplies you have provided, but they do not have to use all of them. They have access to the scissors for cutting the cardboard if they want to and they can use the pencils (or crayons) for decorating the item when finished.

Explain that the items will be judged on imaginativeness of purpose and efficiency of design.

3. Allow each group about 20-30 minutes to decide upon and execute their project.

4. When they have completed the task, each group should be asked to present and explain its creation to the other groups. It is not necessary to decide a winner, but if you want to, allow the students to choose the winning project.

Discussion of Creativity

At this point you can introduce the discussion by asking some of the following questions:

1. Did you think this exercise was hard? Fun? Silly? Interesting? Can you explain why you felt that way?

2. Did you think when you began that you would be able to make anything out of the materials you were given? Do you think that there are many other kinds of things you could make out of the same materials if you really worked at it?

3. Do you think you would have preferred to do this kind of project alone, or were you glad you had a group to work with? Why?

4. When people can see new possibilities in common objects like those you used, we usually say they are creative. Did you feel that you were involved in a creative activity? What do you think creativity is? Do you think any person or group can be creative if they want to?

5. Can people be creative in other ways than just in making things? Can you give examples? Can you think of any persons you know who you feel are creative? In what ways are they creative?

6. Is it possible to "live creatively" rather than just do some things creatively? What would it mean for a high school

student to live creatively? A mother? A butcher?

7. Do you think the college students' reaction to "the Establishment" is a creative one? Why? What are (could be) some creative reactions?

8. Why do you think more people aren't creative? Do you think creativity is a special gift or do you think a person can develop it? Explain.

9. If you think a person can develop creativity, how do you think he can go about doing it?

10. Can people who are afraid of making mistakes be creative? Do you think we hurt the potential for creativity in others by ridiculing them? What's the difference between conformity, creativity, and anarchy?

VALUES

Definition of Values

This topic could be approached from two points of view. Since all values have moral implications, we might say the topic is concerned with morality. On the other hand, since all values serve as motivations for actions, the topic could be interpreted as a study in motivation. In either case, the goal is the same: to help the students become more aware of the values that are operative in their own lives and to help them clarify the hierarchy of values they presently hold.

It has always been surprising to me to discover that many students, while obviously possessing a "set of values" which both motivate them and which they use to judge the right and wrong of their actions, have never critically analyzed these values. Often their values have been acquired gradually, as if through familial and cultural osmosis. The students are not aware that these values have been acquired. To them it seems they have always been there. "That's the way it is," they remark.

The values they consciously hold are usually in direct conflict with those of their parents, their religion or the Establishment — a reflection of their rebellion with the accepted values of the society. Even in this instance, though, students are often not aware of how they acquired these differing values. Again they feel that "that's the way it really is."

Thus, a discussion in values should include two things. First, the conscious awareness of the values that are operative in our lives and the ordering of these values from most important to least important. Second, an examination of how we develop values in the first place. The exercise in this lesson aims primarily at becoming aware of the values we have. Through the discussion that follows, the students should be led to the second question of how values are acquired.

This latter question deserves a little comment. We tend to acquire values on several levels. First, through society — which includes for the student his youth culture of disc jockeys, fads, "what the other kids are doing," etc. In this regard it would make an interesting study if someone were to examine the effects that youth on the east and west coasts have on youth in middle America. It seems that the two coasts (specifically California and New York) initiate much of what eventually becomes "in" in the Midwest a few months later. The fact is that for the adolescent, who is usually rejecting the various norms acquired as a child, many of his values come from his peer culture and from the college culture he aspires to enter. As such, this is neither bad nor good. What is critical is that young people become aware of how greatly they are influenced by this youth culture.

A second source of values lies in the various psychological needs the adolescent experiences, many of which are not conscious. For example, a boy may place a higher value on athletics than on studies because of his need to be considered "manly" by his peers. Or an unattractive girl may place a high value on studies to compensate for her inability to get into the social swing. In these instances, a youth's values may become quite distorted unless he becomes aware of the kinds of psychological needs that are motivating him. This can be treated in general terms in a classroom setting, but specific problems are best handled in a one-to-one counseling situation.

Finally, many of a student's values have been acquired through his family and through his formal religion training. His surface rebellion against some of these does not indicate that he is actually free of them. These values are often more operative than he would care to admit to his parents or to his peers and are often a source of inner conflict and guilt. For example, "down deep" he still may hold to traditional values regarding the importance of religion, but he fears that he would be labeled "pious" if he expressed these values. If students are to be both conscious and critical of their own values, they will have to become aware of these various ways in which they acquire them.

Importance of Values

Since a person's values are at the heart of his actions, the more conscious he is of them the more conscious — and human — will be his actions. That's the rather obvious importance of studying values. More immediate, though, is the fact that our society is undergoing a severe upheaval regarding its own values. The resulting confusion both old and young experience makes a discussion on the nature of values and how they are acquired very timely and helpful. While this topic can help put the whole social question of values into some perspective, it also serves to give the student an opportunity to look at and question his own values.

Problems Related to Values

It is important to keep in mind that the topic deals with the *nature* and *development* of values, not with particular values. Certainly, particular values will have to be discussed by way of example or to demonstrate a point, but the lesson is not intended to indoctrinate students regarding any particular set of values. If you give the impression that this is what you are about, the chances are good that the students will turn you off very quickly. For them values are very personal, even if they haven't thought them through, so you should avoid the idea that you are challenging the values they do have. Rather, you are attempting to create a situation in which they themselves can become more conscious and critical of their values.

Second, since many values have religious origins and overtones, it's important to avoid giving the impression that you are criticizing or promoting a particular religion. While common sense makes this obvious to any experienced teacher, it is good to give yourself a personal reminder, and to make it clear to the students before they become defensive about their own religious beliefs. In some instances I've seen a discussion on values end up in a religious debate, which ruins the chance to achieve the goal intended by the topic.

Finally, it may appear phony to the students to initiate this topic on its own merits. Often it is better to use it after some form of debate has begun around a particular value related to another subject. For example, the students may become very involved in a discussion of the value their parents place on money. In that kind of context it is safe to raise the question of values in general — what we mean by them, the values we have, the order we would place them in, how we acquired them. To start out cold on the topic of values often produces stereotyped responses which the students feel the teacher expects of them. If they begin with a very real question regarding values, their responses later about values in general are more likely to reflect how they actually feel.

Cultivating an Awareness of Values
We've stressed that the lesson does not deal with teaching particular values. Values are acquired or learned through a complex of influences, usually over a long period of time. No one classroom experience is enough to form a person in a particular value. But sometimes one class is sufficient to make the students

more conscious and critical of their values, which is what we hope to achieve. It is after they see the importance of being aware of their values (motives) and how they acquire them, that you can afford to initiate discussion on particular values. Such a discussion is what will keep alive and develop in students a critical awareness of values in general and the influences that shape the formation of their values.

For that reason, it is often best to introduce the general topic of values as early as possible in a course. This can establish a foundation and a framework of common understanding for investigating the particular values which the course deals with throughout the year. Each time a discussion on one of these particular values comes up — e.g., the value of aesthetic appreciation in a course on literature — you are developing a more conscious, critical attitude in students regarding the general question of values in their life.

Suggested Exercise for Experiencing Values

Purpose:

To involve the students in the process of examining their values in a non-threatening way and to open the door for a meaningful discussion of values in general.

Preparation:

If the group is small it is good to gather the actual items listed below so the students have something tangible to work with. However, if you are dealing with a whole class, divide it into several groups of six to eight and give them slips of paper with the name of the items listed below:

> dollar bill
> TV Guide or Movie Guide
> aspirin
> toy gun (to represent real gun)
> car keys

a text book or encyclopedia

a Bible

copy of the Bill of Rights or the Declaration of Independence

a valentine

Instructions:

1. Each group is to first come to an agreement as to what value each of the objects above symbolizes for them. For example, aspirin may symbolize good health, or it may symbolize hallucinogenic drugs. The gun may symbolize power or it may symbolize self-defense.

2. After each group has decided what the objects symbolize in terms of possible values, each individual in the group should arrange the objects according to his own hierarchy of values.

3. Next each group should come to an agreement as to how these objects are to be ordered. This requires that each individual mention his own ordering, and why he followed it.

When several groups are involved, each group can present its list to other groups for comparison, both of interpretation of the symbols and the ordering of the values they represent. It would be interesting to see if any consensus emerges.

Note: There is a great deal of learning that can take place in the groups as they discuss their interpretation of the symbols and the hierarchy of values, so ample time should be provided. Also, their interpretation of symbols can be very enlightening for the teacher.

4. When all the comparing is completed you may want to stimulate further discussion by some of the following questions.

Discussion of Values

1. In discussing the symbolism of the various objects, were you surprised either by the disagreement or agreement of interpretation? For example, that money could be approached in so many different ways?
2. How did you feel when you realized that you were not always in agreement with others? Did you want to convince them of your interpretation or were you eager to agree with them? Could you agree with the final list?
3. How about the ordering of the objects? Did you find it hard coming to agreement? Did you have to back down often? Were you able to convince others of the correctness of your suggestions?
4. Do you think your final ordering of the objects would be acceptable to your parents? In what ways do you think they would differ? Do you think they would have interpreted the symbols differently?
5. How does your list compare with the values presented to you by your parents, or by society at large? Do you find there are any serious differences? How do you feel about that?
6. Do you think others influence you very much in forming the values you have? Who? How? Is this a good influence as far as you are concerned? How do you judge that?
7. Do you think someone from a different culture would come up with a different ordering of the same list of values, for example a Russian? Is this good or bad? Does it indicate anything?
8. Do you think you will change the ordering of these values as you grow older? Why or why not? What would be areas where you doubt if you would ever change?
9. How much do you think our inner needs determine the values that we hold? Do you feel there are some values that are important to you that aren't represented on the list? What are they?
10. Do you think, if we re-arranged the groups and did the exercise again, we would come up with some new values and some new ordering? Why?

FREEDOM AND RESPONSIBILITY

Definition of Freedom and Responsibility
Adolescence is a period of important growth in personal freedom
— a very self-conscious growth, it may be added. Adults, especially parents, witness this growth with a certain uneasiness. For
young people seem to grow unevenly. They are quick to request
(demand) certain rights such as staying out later, making decisions concerning where they go, the companions they keep, the
things they can do. But this rapid growth in concern over freedom does not seem to be accompanied by the same growth in
willingness to assume added responsibilities. A teenage girl may
be quite vocal about her right to decide whom she is going to
date, but can be quite careless about her housekeeping chores. As
soon as a boy is old enough to legally drive he is quick to seek his
own car or at least free access to the family car. Yet he seems
oblivious to his responsibilities to help care for his younger
brother or sister.

These minor domestic contradictions between a demand for
freedom and a willingness to share responsibility become more
dramatic when we view youth in general. For example their
demand to participate in forming school policy is often not
accompanied by a concern for taking proper care of school
property. This same kind of contradiction is pointed out by
national leaders and college administrators in regard to college

students' protests for more freedom on the one hand and their disrespect for civil law on the other.

The tug between freedom and responsibility is as old as adolescence itself, and a standard measure of maturity is the person's capacity to balance personal freedom with personal responsibility in the use of that freedom. The goal of this topic is to help students become more aware of this conflict within themselves and the need to acquire personal balance between freedom and responsibility.

It is normal for the desire for freedom to develop faster than the ability to assume responsibility. It also seems more healthy, since the person who goes through adolescence surrounded by the high walls of rules and inescapable responsibilities and who never has a chance to get a real feel for personal freedom has little chance of developing into a self-directed and truly responsible person. He will develop into an automaton who often harbors a deep resentment for authority, or he himself becomes an intolerable authoritarian.

It is good to note that youth are usually willing to assume responsibility once they are confident that adults are sincere in extending greater freedom to them. Anyone who has witnessed — with a certain ambivalence — the transition of a traditional school into an ungraded school or a modular programmed schedule with contractual course work has discovered that after the initial chaos and some slippage in performance, students accept the new responsibilities and usually fare much better academically. Once they are assured that you really are giving them freedom, they begin to realize that they are truly responsible for how well they use it. They can no longer pass the blame to anyone else.

So there is no need to be alarmed that youth are more eager for freedom than they seem to be for responsibility. There is a need, however, to help them see that the two qualities are complimentary. We cannot have true freedom if we are unwilling to

48

accept responsibility for the use of that freedom. Nor can we be truly responsible if we are not truly free.

Importance of Freedom and Responsibility

The imbalance between freedom and responsibility seems to be at the heart of the traditional adult-youth conflict and mutual distrust. The balance of the two seems to be the basis for a healthy, mature personality. Anything that a teacher can do to speed up the student's acquisition of this balance is important. Not only would it help the student to grow, it would also aid in healing some of the wounds suffered in the generation gap.

It should be added that our whole system of government rests upon the exercise and preservation of responsible freedom. It's at the heart of the democratic process. Facism and anarchy — over-emphasis on responsibility and over-emphasis on freedom — represent the two extremes which destroy democracy. In the light of the violence and social conflict our country has experienced the past several years, this topic becomes a rather critical one. And not just for adolescents, but for adults as well.

Problems Related to Freedom and Responsibility

In discussing this topic with students, I've found the biggest problem to be their shortsightedness. They live very much for the present and can't become too excited over long-range goals or the long-range effects of their actions. This results in an inability to see the full implications of what they do or refuse to do. Yet responsible action requires this kind of long view and circumspection. For example, they have a hard time seeing why a mother would be so uptight just because they are a half-hour late for supper. They have a hard time realizing how much this may inconvenience others who have plans of their own, or how distressful it is to see a good roast shrivel and dry up in the warming oven. This is even more true when it comes to matters like studies, experimenting with sex, drugs and alcohol or fast driving.

What tends to be important is the present moment. If it is pleasant and adventuresome, it is hard for young people to realize that long-range consequences may be disastrous. So the problem is not so much one of convincing them that they should use their freedom responsibly. It centers more on getting them to recognize that present actions, which seem very harmless, can be very irresponsible when viewed in terms of their full effects on themselves and others.

A second problem, more current in society today, is the fact that our culture does not afford the student with "relevant" responsibilities. We expect them to study; that's their present responsibility. We expect them to empty the garbage and make their bed and get home on time; that's their responsibility. We expect them to obey civil laws and school rules; that's their responsibility. But there is little room in our present political or cultural system for them to help shape policy or improve social conditions. To do this they must take to the streets and protest, an action adults are quick to judge irresponsible because of the inevitable rowdiness and the potential destruction that it involves.

So in speaking to students about responsibility, you can anticipate their objections. To them it seems they are still treated like children — which in one sense they are. Our culture seems to prefer that we find a way to keep them harmlessly preoccupied until they are about twenty-five, have learned a skill or profession and are ready to settle down and conform to society's norms. We are prolonging irresponsibility because we are hesitant to give youth a share in the real responsibilities of developing our society and solving its problems. And young people resent this deeply. Dropping out, drugs, violent protest are just a few symptoms of this resentment. They are styles of responsibility in reverse. Though motivated by a real desire to be responsible persons and to assume responsibility within society, their actions produce results which our society considers destructive and therefore, irresponsible. It is similar to the small child who picks mother's prize rose and then presents it to her proudly as a gift. The mother may be disappointed by the result of the action, but she is deeply touched by the motive that inspired it. Therefore, any serious discussion of freedom and responsibility will have to confront this problem.

Another rather common reaction of youth to this topic has been their criticism of what they consider childish or ir-responsible actions in adults. Some of this criticism is usually emotional and exaggerated, a defensive move to protect themselves by blaming others. But some of it is also accurate and perceptive. The teacher will have to deal with these criticisms honestly to avoid turning the students off.

Cultivating an Awareness of Freedom and Responsibility

If there were one simple way to help young people acquire a balance between their rightful freedom and the responsible use of it, we would simultaneously annihilate the adolescent stage of development and solve the problem of moral formation. There is no simple formula. The school of life teaches this lesson negative-ly: our past mistakes point up the relationship between our free acts and undesirable consequences. If you don't study, you fail the course. If you don't watch your diet, no one watches your figure. The unfortunate thing about this type of education is that sometimes, by the time you learn the lesson, it is too late to benefit by it.

A more positive way to learn this lesson is through developing the habit of "looking and feeling in all directions." This can be done in a more structured way than the "school of life" method. It means that we pick out a single decision and think through all its possible consequences. To teach this kind of reflection it is good to suggest that students think through four categories of consequences: the personal good that may result;

the good that may result for others; the personal harm that may result; the harm that others may experience because of the action. In each category the student should try to anticipate all the *possible* results, not just immediate, but long-range.

Suppose, for instance, that a student wants to skip class to attend a peace demonstration. He ought to consider the personal harm of possible suspension from school or the anger that will be engendered at home if his parents disapprove of such actions. Then there are the good results of living out his convictions, of participating in an event which could possibly create a better world, or of being with people who feel the same way he does. When it comes to the possible good or harm to others, it is important that students try to enter into the feelings of others as well as the external effects they may experience. For example, how does a school principal feel when placed in the position of having to mete out punishment. Such feelings are all part of the effect of the action and must be considered in deciding upon it.

This kind of approach can be taken both with theoretical decisions and with decisions students have already made. In either case, it tends to make them more aware of the big picture, something we said earlier adolescents are not prone to examine unless they are educated to do so.

The particular exercise we are suggesting in connection with this topic is intended to focus students on the problem of freedom vs. responsibility. Consideration of actions like attending a demonstration will have meaning for them once they become more aware of the problem itself.

Suggested Exercise for Experiencing Freedom and Responsibility
Purpose:
   To give the students an experience of the tug between their personal freedom to pursue their own interests and their responsibility to others.

Preparation:

No props are required.

Divide students into groups of six or eight; if you have only one group, divide it in half.

Arrange groups in straight lines, one person behind the other.

Instructions:

1. Explain that the exercise is intended to measure each person's capacity for group loyalty while at the same time being a measure of a person's endurance.

2. Each person is to remain silent and to face forward at all times. The exercise is to be done in silence.

3. Arrange each group in a row, one person behind the other. Tell them to lift their arms out sideways until level with their shoulders. They are to hold them in that position.

   If a person lowers his arms, his entire group is eliminated. The exercise is to continue until only one group remains. This group has proven greater loyalty and endurance than the others.

   Note: This exercise should be continued until it is obviously "hurting," but if you judge that someone may be too embarrassed by letting down his group, there is no need to continue it until one group remains. The actual elimination process does add considerably more dynamism to the exercise, however. If you do the latter, your task is to call out that a group is eliminated when you see someone lower his arms.

   When one group is left or after you have called the exercise to a halt, you can begin the discussion, remembering that the real concern is the conflict between freedom and responsibility to others.

Discussion of Freedom and Responsibility

1. Each person actually had the right to lower his arms when it became painful. What was your reason for keeping them up? Did you feel any real responsibility to the others even though it meant pain for you?

2. Did the task become more difficult because you could not see the faces of the persons in your group? Do you think being toward the rear of the line made it different than being near the front or in the front?

3. Were you afraid of what the others in your group would say if you let them down? Is this kind of fear a rather common reason for doing things you don't particularly want to do? Are there other motives besides fear?

4. When one of the other groups was eliminated, did you feel that you now had greater responsibility to keep your arms up? Why? Did you feel that you had lost your freedom to lower your arms? Did you in fact lose your freedom? Explain?

5. If your group was eliminated, were you upset by the person who lowered his arms, or did you sympathize with him because of your own experience of pain? Were you perhaps actually grateful that someone else lowered his arms because then you could lower yours without fear of embarrassment?

6. This was a very artificial situation created only to make a point. What do you think was the real point or points in the exercise?

7. Can you think of any real-life situations you've been in where you've experienced a similar pull between your personal rights and your responsibility to others?

8. Are there ever any kinds of situations in which your exercise of personal freedom is not somehow connected with a responsibility to others? For example?

9. What are the options you face in situations in which your right to do your own thing may at the same time be irresponsible in terms of its effects on others?

10. Are there times when it is better to go along with the group than to do your own thing? Such as?

RESPECT

Definition of Respect

According to its etymology, respect means to "look back" or to "take a second look." This implies that the first impression of the person viewed was positive and encouraging. When understood this way, the real burden is upon the one viewed. He must make such a good first impression that others will "re-spect" him. As we are using the word in this chapter, however, the burden is placed on the viewer rather than the one viewed. In doing so, we are making a very crucial assumption: every person, by virtue of his being a person, demands our initial attention.

If you accept this assumption, at least as a working principle, respect means a habit of approaching each person you meet with good will and an open mind. Respect, then, is a kind of positive prejudice, an initial trust in the goodness of others. In this sense respect is initially a reflex action or an habitual attitude toward others in general. It becomes a deliberate attitude toward an individual person later, as our initial act of trust is supported by the good we experience in him.

This may sound like we are making a simple concept complicated, but it is important to realize that respect as used in this chapter is treated as a desired *initial attitude toward others*, and not as something that we win from others by our good actions or talents. That is why we prefer to define it as a positive prejudice, or open-mindedness, or good will which we exercise toward others, no matter who they may be or when we meet them. Respect in this sense is the opposite of negative prejudice which judges people badly, based only on external characteristics or initial impressions. (We will deal with prejudice as a distinct topic in Chapter 7.)

To respect everyone in this way is not illogical, however, in the way that an actual prejudice is illogical. The ability to respect every human being is based on the conviction that mankind is basically good and deserving of our respect. This conviction may be supported by religious belief, by philosophy or by wide experience in dealing with others, such as the kind a counselor has. On a more personal level, each of us experiences a deep feeling that we deserve – and need – the respect of others, even given our faults.

Regardless of how this conviction is supported, though, it is essential if society is to function. Respect, as a basic attitude toward others, is the absolute minimum that is necessary *before* any constructive human relationships can take place. If a person does not approach others with at least some minimal respect for them, the other is automatically, if unconsciously, placed in the category of an "it" or an "enemy." Consequently, no authentic communication can take place. The attitude of respect for others is the first door we must walk through in our effort to live in restful and peaceful human relationships.

Perhaps this becomes more evident when we recognize situations in which this kind of respect is lacking. In it most extreme form, the inability to respect others is found in paranoid persons. Living in fear and suspicion of everyone around him, the paranoid person can form positive relationships with no one. He is literally cut off from human communication. Worse, he is potentially a dangerous force, first to himself, and then to others. For the paranoid person, negative prejudice is a way of life.

In more common experiences, the teacher who is suspicious

or disrespectful of his students is defeated before he begins. Students may perform for him, but they will never learn since the basis for real communication has been destroyed at the outset. The child who lacks respect for the elderly or for his parents has put himself out of touch with them. He has cut himself off from whatever good they have to share with him as persons because he has a closed mind in their regard. This same pattern becomes very visible in high school settings when students set themselves up in cliques and view other groups or individuals as not worthy of their respect. While granting the harm done to the individuals who are scorned, the real harm is done to the one who fails to respect others. His closed mind keeps cutting him off from reality. He becomes trapped within his small world.

Much more common than the kinds of disrespect just mentioned above is our tendency to categorize people, to put them in boxes or give them labels based on some external appearance. The reason for this is obvious enough. It is a simple way to resolve the problems of relating to people. As soon as we can label them we have solved the problem of how to treat them. We say for example "All long-hairs are hippies." We see a person with long hair and beads. We label him hippie, which may or may not be accurate. And with the label goes all that we consider every hippie to be. We aren't forced to consider that there may be "good hippies" and "bad hippies." That would complicate matters and we would have to deal with each one individually. This tendency to categorize is often a form of interpersonal laziness rather than the narrow-mindedness we call prejudice, but it has the same basic effect.

Adolescents often feel that adults categorize all teenagers in one bag, which we often do, with comments like "kids today don't want to work" or "kids today just don't respect property." Naturally adolescents resent this. They are at a stage of development where it is crucial for them to feel like individuals, and they rightly consider such categorizing as a form of disrespect for their person.

Young people, of course, are prone to do the same thing toward parents, or police, or teachers. Thus, in the process of discussion, this kind of disrespect should be brought out. They should be reminded that one of our chief motives for categorizing people is not bad will as much as it is a desire to simplify the problem of relating to them.

Importance of Respect

Because this habitual positive attitude toward others is the foundation of all truly human relationships, the need that it be understood by students appears evident. Respect, as was mentioned earlier, is the counter attitude to prejudice. And in a society like ours, where it is increasingly more important that people in large numbers learn to live harmoniously in close proximity, respect is the essential foundation for that harmony. Many of our immediate problems — generation gap, racial hatred, vandalism, crimes of violence, student rebellion — have the roots of their solution in an understanding of what it really means to respect others. What the world needs now is not "love, sweet love." That's a luxury few can afford. Just the ability to say "I believe you have goodness within you" to our fellow human beings — and then treat them accordingly — would be a sufficient beginning.

Problems Related to Respect

The real problem with respect is to make it concrete enough for students to grasp what you are asking of them as a life-style. Speaking in general terms about something like respect seems either to have little application in daily life, or to be idealistic to the point of unreality. That is why it is important to continuously stress that respect is basically open-mindedness toward others, a minimal trust in their goodness. The school janitor deserves this much. So does the salesclerk at the supermarket, the over-weight student, and the old lady who works in the cafeteria; not to mention parents, brothers and sisters, neighbors, class-mates. So the first problem is to make respect something real and possible in the students' lives. The idea of open-mindedness will appeal to them.

The second problem, perhaps more difficult, is that students will often expect some immediate results for their actions. If they trust a person in a respectful way, they want to be reciprocated. If they say a friendly "hello" to the janitor and he growls back at them, so much for respecting the janitor. Thus it is important to help students understand that respect isn't based on externals or on nice words or a helpful gesture. Either the janitor is a human being and deserves respect or he is some kind of monster and should be shunned if not locked up. Assuming he is a human being, respect for him doesn't depend on how he acts today or tomorrow. It depends on who he is. It means trying to under-stand that paper on the floor is aggravating to him, and walls that are all marked up make him miserable. If we want friendly words from someone, it is not enough that we use friendly words our-selves. We must enter into that person's life and discover what he really needs to make him happy. Friendly words come after we have respected the other person's needs and at least not hindered him in fulfilling them.

Cultivating Respect

Since every person both needs and desires the respect of others, the real foundation for building the habit of respect lies within the individual. It is first necessary to help the student recognize just how much he depends upon the respect of others and just how bad he feels when it is not given to him. He should also be helped to reflect upon his reaction when he feels he is not

59

respected — how he withdraws from the person who has not respected him on the one hand, or attacks him on the other. Drawing upon this personal experience and the feelings and actions it evokes, it is not hard to help the student realize that others feel and react the same way when he fails to respect them, whether it's his father, a classmate or some bus driver he encounters on the way home. In this way there builds up in the student's mind an appreciation for the nature and importance of respect in his daily life.

The next step is to give him a "target" to practice on. For example, encourage the student to pick out some person whom he would normally not respect. Ask the student to focus on this person, try to "get inside him" attempt to discover what he is really like by observing him, talking to him, associating with him. At the same time, the student should try to treat this other person in a friendly, considerate way, either by words or by deeds. And he should be reminded not to expect immediate friendliness in return. If he stays with this effort for a reasonable time, say several weeks or a month, and he keeps an open mind, there is an excellent chance he will discover that he really can respect the person whom he initially had no use for. While he is doing this, he is at the same time becoming more conscious of being respectful in general. This becomes the beginning of the habit of respect — a life-style of open-mindedness and good will toward those whom he meets.

Suggested Exercise for Experiencing Respect
Purpose:

> To help students feel what it is like not to be respected and to recognize the kinds of reactions it evokes in them, thus creating a situation in which the nature and importance of respect can be discussed.

Preparation:

Ask a friend, ideally someone whom the students do not know or have little contact with, to help you in this exercise. The students are told that this person is coming to give a talk on some topic that is related to what you are treating in class. Do not mention that you plan to introduce the topic of respect.

Instructions:

1. Your friend is instructed to go through the motions of talking on the announced subject but to be as insulting and disrespectful as he can to the students. For example, he could begin by saying, "You probably aren't intelligent enough to follow what I am going to say, but I will try to explain it to you." He might single out individual students to whom he can direct insulting comments, and in general be obnoxious. It would be good if he made some categorizing statements, like "Since you're kids, you probably aren't interested in any serious questions." Or "You're not paying attention to what I'm saying. That's the trouble with you kids, no respect for your elders." At the same time he should try not to be too obvious about what he is doing.

2. After he has aroused sufficient feelings in the students (and before you have a riot on your hands) you can interrupt the speaker and direct a question at one of the students most provoked, such as: "John, how do you feel about the way Mr. Smith has been treating the students in this class?" If properly encouraged that you are on his side at this point, John will give an honest answer regarding his anger. You may ask for comments from one or two others, and then explain that the whole effort was a "put on" in order to give them an immediate experience of what it feels like to be disrespected.

3. You can then begin the general discussion with some of the following questions. The guest speaker may stay and join in.

Discussion of Respect

1. What were your first reactions when you began to feel that the speaker was not respecting you? Anger, embarrassment for him, indifference?
2. As he continued, were you able to pay attention to what he was saying or had he "turned you off"? Did you feel he had put you in a box or had already labeled you without first getting to know you personally?
3. Have you ever been treated this way as an individual? By whom? How did you feel?
4. Is the kind of attitude the speaker displayed rather common today in society? Do adults in general disrespect high school students? How about the way high school students treat adults? Who is to blame?
5. Since the speaker really didn't know any of you, did you feel he was very unfair and prejudiced in the way he was treating you? Is this a normal way to treat people you don't know?
6. Do high school students often treat each other in the same way before they get to know each other? Why?
7. We had a good example of what it feels like to be disrespected. Can you think of times when someone respected you before he really knew you? Can you give examples? How did you feel and react then?
8. What do you think respect really is? What do you think is necessary before you can respect someone?
9. Why does it often happen that in a group, high school students can give someone like a bus driver a hard time, but when each student is alone he can be very nice to people, even strangers?
10. What would happen if you began to respect everyone you met? Would you be taken? Would you get hurt? Can you really respect everyone you meet?

TRUST

Definition of Trust

Any teacher who's worked with adolescents knows how guarded they can be around adults and around other adolescents they don't know — even in this age of openness and "telling it like it is." This unwillingness to expose themselves — what they really think and feel — can be attributed to their own uncertainty about themselves. They can't begin to trust other people, they can't begin to risk mistakes or "saying something foolish" until they have begun to trust themselves.

Trust, as we are using it, means this ability to risk yourself, to put yourself in the hands of another, to put yourself at the service of another. And you just don't do that until you own yourself, that is, until you have enough self-confidence and self-possession that you can afford to "let yourself go." Trust is always a risk, a kind of leap in the dark. It is not based on any solid proof that the other person will not hurt you. If you have that kind of proof, you are dealing with a sure thing, and trust is always a gamble. That's why the capacity to trust comes from inside, not outside. The "sure thing" is your own worth, your own certainty in yourself, not the certainty you have in another. That comes later — *after* you've trusted someone and he has not let you down.

From what we are saying, it should be clear that we are not

dealing with the kind of trust a child has in his parents or the trust a religious person places in his God. Such trust is based on the manifest goodness or trustworthiness of the person trusted; it is evoked from without. The capacity to trust that we are concerned with is an inner quality of emotional maturity and it affects all human relationships, not just specialized ones.

To trust, then, is to take the initiative, to make the first step toward another, to hold out your hand, to say "I like you" before you are sure what the other person will say in return. This naturally leads to the question: How does a person go about gaining the kind of self-confidence that enables him to trust others? From others. Others have to convince us that we are good. That's the essential job of parents. It's the role of friendship. And should be the role of education, too.

Family, friends and teachers are primary sources of a student's self-image. If that combination of influences helps a person discover his own worth, he in turn will be in a position to trust others, to go out to them and in the process help others discover their own worth. That seems to be what human relations are all about — helping each other respect ourselves to the point where we can afford to give of ourselves to others.

Nobody is going to discover his own worth overnight. That's a long process; it's called "growing up." But at least it is possible to help students realize the importance of being able to trust others and to realize that it depends on how they regard themselves.

Importance of Trust

This should be rather self-evident. Trust, like respect, is basic to human relationships. Trust just goes one step further than respect. To respect someone is to give him the benefit of the doubt, to assume that he is basically good. To trust someone is to get involved, to act out your respect, to risk yourself to some degree. So if respect is the foundation for human relationships, trust is the relationship itself. For these reasons, students should grasp the significance of trust. But more important they should become aware of their own ability or inability to trust.

Problems Related to Trust

Since adolescents are naturally unsure of themselves, it's necessary to keep in mind that you can't force a person to trust any more than you can force a person to recognize his own worth. So, in dealing with the topic, realize that the goal is not so much to teach a person to trust. Rather it is to teach them about trust and help them experience what it feels like to trust, or not be able to trust.

Most students will have rather concrete ideas about trust. It means to lend a buddy your car because you trust him, or tell a friend a secret because you trust her. They ordinarily don't approach it as a life-style that applies to human relations in general. So it will be necessary to get them thinking in this more general way at some point in your discussion or they can miss the point entirely.

Finally, since trust is based on self-confidence, and this is a topic that students are understandably touchy about, I've found it is a good idea to talk about trust and self-confidence in relative terms. That is, we all have self-confidence to a degree — the more we have the better — and we keep growing in it all our lives. The same is true of our ability to trust. In other words, avoid giving the students an absolute standard to measure themselves against right now. Give them a long-range goal to shoot for as a normal process of maturing. Make it clear that no one is expected at any particular stage in life to reach the ideal. And certainly you are not expecting perfect maturity of them at their present age.

Cultivating Trust

Since trust depends upon the student's developing self-image, it cannot be directly taught. The only thing you can do — other than your normal attempts to help develop a healthy self-image in your students — is to help them see the relationship between their own self-confidence and their ability to "get involved" with others. Everyone has a natural desire to form human relationships; you don't have to teach that. You can help students recognize the necessary role trust plays in this desire. The rest will be up to them.

Suggested Exercise for Experiencing Trust

Purpose:

> To give the students an insight based on their own self-confidence into their ability to trust others, and thus to create a situation in which meaningful discussion concerning the nature and necessity of trust can take place.

Preparation:

> Each student should be given a copy of the following list:
>> Imitate the crowing of a rooster.
>>
>> Give a two-minute talk about your best qualities.
>>
>> Do a silent pantomime of a very sleepy person brushing his teeth.
>>
>> Give a two-minute talk on what you like most about your classmates.
>>
>> Recite a short nursery rhyme you remember from your childhood.
>>
>> Balance a book on your head and walk across the room.
>>
>> Read a short passage of your choice from a book that is available in the room.

Instructions:

> 1. The exercise should be introduced as an activity to

measure their ability to trust others, without mentioning that this is also a measure of self-confidence.

2. Ask each student to number the activities on his list from one to seven, in order of what he would most prefer doing in front of the group to what he would least prefer doing. Explain that any individual may be called upon to actually perform one of his first three choices, so they will give serious thought to how they order the choices.

3. When everyone has completed his list, ask by a show of hands how many put "imitate a rooster" first, and how many put it last. Do the same with each item, recording the results. When you have the numbers recorded, then go through the list again, asking someone who put the item as his first choice to actually perform the activity. Skip any item that no one chose for his first choice so as not to embarrass anyone.

4. After the performances are over (these need not take long since they have no value in themselves but merely serve to keep the exercise "honest") you can initiate discussion. Give the statistics about which activities were chosen first and last and ask the students to comment why they think certain items were rated the way they were. From this point you will want to get into the main concern of the topic by using some of the following questions.

Discussion of Trust

1. Did you feel uneasy about the whole idea of possibly having to perform one of the items on the list?

2. Do you think everyone listed the items in order of the least to the most embarrassing to do in front of a group? Is this a usual reaction?

3. In what way do you think the ordering of the list is an indication of our ability to trust others? Is it also a measure of how we trust ourselves? Why?

4. Is it safer to do something silly in a group like an imitation of a rooster, than it is to do something serious like talk about your own good qualities? Why?

5. How did you feel when you realized that you would not have to perform? (Applies when a group is large enough that some did not perform.)

6. Are our ability to trust others and our ability to trust ourselves two aspects of the same thing? Can you explain what you mean? Is this kind of trust different than the trust we exercise when we lend someone money or share a secret?

7. What would happen in a group like this if no one was able to trust others except in superficial things like imitating a rooster? Are there situations you've been in where matters never get beyond the level of silliness? What is it like? What do you think is the reason for it? What would it take to overcome that kind of situation?

8. How does a person go about developing greater self-confidence? Can we help each other become more self-confident? Can we destroy someone's self-confidence? In what ways? How would destroying someone's self-confidence affect his ability to relate to others?

9. Do you think much confidence-building takes place among your peers? Does the destroying of self-confidence take place? Can you give examples?

10. Is part of the reason why young people don't always trust adults due to the fact that they (the young people) have not yet learned to really trust themselves?

After the discussion you may want to summarize the key points and mention those not covered.

PREJUDICE

Definition of Prejudice

Prejudice means just what the Latin root and prefix suggest: to pre-judge, to make up your mind ahead of time, to decide *before* you have studied the facts. In itself to pre-judge is not bad. In many instances it is necessary. For example, in an emergency situation a person may have to make a decision before he can study all the facts. Also, intuition is a kind of pre-judgment; a person sees the entire situation in a flash and makes a judgment without bothering to logically analyze all the details. We even regard an intuitive person as gifted. Nor does prejudice necessarily mean thinking evil of another person. You can have a positive prejudice; you can decide you like a person before you have really come to know all the details about him.

Prejudice becomes a fault and takes on the connotations suggested in a term like "racial prejudice" only when certain other qualities are present. First, it is a fault when it indicates a lack of logic. For example the person making a snap decision and the intuitive person are still operating logically; they are just taking short cuts. A "prejudiced person" on the other hand, is illogical. He is drawing the wrong conclusions from the evidence available, or, more accurately, he is drawing conclusions without looking at the evidence.

Second, prejudice becomes a fault when it threatens the

rights of others. For example, a person may be prejudiced against oysters. He judges their taste only by their appearance and refuses to eat them. Such an action is illogical in that we can only judge the taste of oysters by tasting them. But it doesn't harm anyone (unless you happen to sell oysters). If, however, we judged a political candidate by the way he dresses or by his racial background or by his diction in public speaking, instead of by his past performance in situations of public responsibility, we are treating him – and the general public whom he seeks to serve – unfairly.

Third, for prejudice to be a fault, it must imply a kind of permanence, an unwillingness or inability to change our attitude, a closed-mindedness. This more than anything else is the diagnostic symptom of the character fault of prejudice. A person can make illogical decisions; these decisions may cause harm to others. But so long as he is always willing (able) to listen to new evidence and change his mind when properly challenged to do so, he is not really a prejudiced person. He may not always be circumspect and logical in the kinds of decisions he makes but he is not prejudiced.

To be a prejudiced person then, is to make illogical decisions which harm others without being able or willing to reconsider the decision if additional evidence presents itself. This can serve as a working definition for a person who has racial prejudice, class prejudice, political prejudice or religious prejudice – the kinds sociologists speak of. Other kinds of prejudice, for example, against oysters or rock music or long hair on boys, may be harmless in themselves, but they are dangerous in that they reinforce the habit of prejudice. This can prepare a person for more socially unacceptable prejudices, or strengthen him in those he has. A bona fide prejudiced person, possessing the three characteristics described above, is actually neurotic if we define neurosis as a distorted view of reality which is not recognized as such by the person possessing it, or which he cannot correct even though he

70

does recognize it. Racial prejudice, as it exists in this country for example, is often described as a collective neurosis.

Prejudice cannot be corrected by reason alone. It requires a kind of therapy. Something like racial prejudice is usually acquired unnoticed, a part of the total environment and culture one accepts as a child. In this sense it is "inherited," is constantly reinforced in childhood, and is already functioning as an integral part of a person's life before he has reached his teens. To challenge this kind of prejudice, for example a person's pre-judgment regarding a particular race of people, is to challenge the total person and his total view of reality. To re-examine this particular judgment he would have to re-examine his entire life up to the present. Because such a task is too overwhelming, a person with a deep-seated prejudice cannot be "convinced by reason" that it is a prejudice in the first place. In fact, by the time a person is in his teens, his racial prejudice is protected by a whole set of "reasons and experiences" which justify his attitude. So it is not enough to challenge a particular prejudice in a person. Rather we must examine the nature of prejudice itself, discover how it insinuates itself into a person's life, recognize that it is a distortion of reality. Once a person is willing to admit that prejudice as such is bad, and can admit that he is capable of prejudice, he can ask "Am I prejudiced?" In other words, we have to challenge prejudice as a life-style before we can challenge a particular prejudice.

Importance of Understanding Prejudice

Racial prejudice is perhaps the single most harmful social disease present in American society. That alone justifies any teacher's efforts to broaden the students' understanding of the nature of prejudice. If you add to that the myriad other kinds of prejudice that cripple people's lives — religious, ideological, social, geographical — and the fact that prejudice by nature is unrecognized by those it infects,. an understanding of prejudice becomes as

71

important as an understanding of the democratic process.

It might be added that high school seems an ideal time to deal with prejudice. During this period young people are naturally involved in re-evaluating themselves and what they have been told as children. They are ripe for re-education. Equally important, their natural idealism makes them quick to see the evils of prejudice, its phoniness, its hypocrisy. The trick though is not to convince them of the evil of prejudice but to help them realize that they are capable of it — and are perhaps already prejudiced in certain areas. That is the real goal of this topic.

Problems Related to Prejudice
The most obvious problem involves the nature of prejudice itself. As we said, you can seldom attack a particular prejudice head on and deal with it logically. To do so merely creates defensiveness and hostility in the prejudiced person. So anyone dealing with the topic of prejudice should approach it in general terms, at least at first.

Second, there is the problem of being prejudiced about prejudice. It is such a common subject today that many will feel they know all there is to know about it. In other words, many people have already pre-judged the nature of prejudice and have formed strong opinions about it. The teacher should be aware of this possibility in his students. It is often necessary to "sneak up" on students and get them involved in the topic before they are aware that the topic is prejudice. The suggested exercise attempts to do this.

Finally, it is good to keep in mind that deep-seated prejudices do have the qualities of a neurosis and that a person often "cannot help himself." This is mentioned because it is very easy to lose patience in the face of a prejudice that is socially unacceptable. The temptation to confrontation or argumentation will be strong, whereas sympathy and tolerance are needed if any real progress is to be made. This is true when dealing with an individual student or a whole roomful of students.

Cultivating an Understanding of Prejudice
The description of the nature of prejudice and of the problems a teacher faces in dealing with it dictate to a large degree the way to present the topic. First, it is best to lead the students to discover themselves in an act of prejudice. This immediately disarms them and demonstrates that everyone is prone to prejudice. From here it is good to discuss prejudice in all its forms and degrees: good prejudices like intuition and acceptance of others, harmless prejudices like having a hang-up on oysters or sardines, prejudices that result from the cultural role of the sexes (eg. boys are prejudiced against poetry because it seems unmanly).

From here it is good to go into more depth about the nature of unacceptable prejudice: its illogical base, its harmfulness to others, the permanence of the decision and the person's blindness to it. In this same context you can discuss how people acquire prejudices, often through their family or their culture, and how they can avoid developing prejudices. It is especially important to stress that a healthy person is always willing to re-examine judgments he has made in the past and maintains an open mind regarding others' opinions.

It seems that only after this kind of exploration has taken place can the teacher successfully bring up particular areas like racial prejudice. While these phenomena can be reviewed objectively, the student is now in a position to make a personal application. He has reached the point where he can afford to ask if he has any prejudices he has not noticed before — without feeling like he is some kind of monster.

Finally, as a counter to the tendency to prejudice it is good to point out its opposite: deliberated honesty. "Deliberated" in that a person weighs the facts available which affect the judgment

73

he is going to make. "Honesty" in that he remains open to truth no matter where it is found or how it demands personal effort or generosity. A person who is deliberately honest is prudent without being suspicious; he is open to change without vacillating. It seems good to leave students with such a positive goal to strive for after you have examined something as negative as prejudice.

Suggested Exercise for Experiencing Prejudice
Purpose:

> To involve the students in an activity which will demonstrate that we all have prejudices, thus opening up the opportunity to discuss the nature of prejudice in a personal rather than a theoretical way.

Preparation:

> Each student should be supplied with a single sheet of paper and a pencil. The paper should be folded in half lengthwise. Take a small box, perhaps the size of a shoe box, and place in it any object, valuable or useless (eg. your watch, a wornout ballpoint pen). Then wrap the box, either in a fancy way like a gift or in a careless way with newspaper and string.

Instructions:

> Explain to the students that you are going to give them a "psychological test," but do not explain what the test is meant to measure. Assure them, however, that it is a fun test and is not intended to embarrass anyone. Tell them that you are going to ask a series of questions and they are to answer them as honestly as they can, using the paper supplied to write the answers, and numbering them in the order given. The questions are these:
> 1. Do you like cats? Answer *yes, no* or *uncertain.*
> 2. Do you like raw oysters? Answer *yes, no* or *uncertain.*
> 3. Do you like classical music? Answer *yes, no* or *uncertain.*

4. Would you like to live in Europe? Answer *yes, no* or *uncertain*.
5. Do you like to waltz? Answer *yes, no* or *uncertain*.
6. Would you like to know what is in this package I am holding up? Answer *yes, no* or *uncertain*.

Now ask them to turn the paper over and answer the following questions, which are the second part of the above questions:

1. Have you ever owned a cat for more than a month? *Yes* or *No*.
2. Have you ever eaten raw oysters? *Yes* or *No*.
3. Have you ever attended a symphony or listened to a complete recording of one? *Yes* or *No*.
4. Have you ever been to Europe? *Yes* or *No*.
5. Do you know how to waltz? *Yes* or *No*.
6. Do you think there is something valuable in this package. Answer *Yes, No* or *Uncertain*.

When they have written their answers, have the students unfold the paper so both sets of answers are visible. To score the test they are to use the following procedure:

1. They get a zero if the second part of the question was answered *no* and the first part was answered either *yes* or *no*.

    Eg. Do you like cats? *Yes*. (Or *No*)
    Have you ever owned a cat for more than a month? *No*.

2. They get one point if they answered the second part of the question *yes* and the first part was answered either *yes* or *no*.

    Eg. Do you like cats? *Yes*. (Or *No*)
    Have you ever owned a cat for more than a month? *Yes*.

3. They get two points if they answered the second part of

75

the question *no* and answered the first part *uncertain*.

    Eg. Do you like cats? *Uncertain*.

       Have you ever owned a cat for more than a month? *No*.

4. They get three points if they answered the second part of the question *yes* and the first part of the question *uncertain*.

    Eg. Do you like cats? *Uncertain*.

       Have you ever owned a cat for more than a month? *Yes*.

Each pair of questions is scored in this way, except for the last question regarding the box. Regardless of how they answer the first part of the last question, they receive a zero if they answer either *yes* or *no* to the second part and three points if they answer *uncertain*. (The question was: Do you think there is something valuable in this package?)

After everyone has totaled his score, announce the following rankings:

15-18 - very open-minded, honest, willing to study the facts

14-10 - average

  9-5 - below average, likely to jump to conclusions, prone to prejudice

  4-0 - very prone to prejudice, easily influenced by opinion of others, or by externals

At this point, students will want to challenge the validity of the test, qualify their answers, question the implications. When this happens you can begin the discussion with some of the suggested questions.

Discussion of Prejudice

1. Can you really judge something if you have had little or no experience of it? Can you judge the taste of an oyster by its

appearance? The beauty of music without seriously listening to it?

2. You have probably heard a statement like this: "I love kittens but I can't stand cats." I think if I were a cat I would resent it because it indicates a prejudgment of all cats. Can you think of any other similar clichés, but ones which deal with people, for example, the American Indian? What effect if any do such statements have on a person who has never met an Indian? Are you aware of having formed any judgments about a group of people based not on personal contact but on such slogans?

3. Jumping to conclusions based on first impressions or on the hearsay evidence of a friend is rather common. Is it a good habit? Can you think of possible dangers in it? What is the difference between taking a friend's word for something — that is, trust — and being gullible?

4. Is forming rash conclusions illogical? When isn't it illogical? Is it a good habit?

5. What's the difference between forming a rash conclusion about oysters or cats and doing the same thing to a person? What do we usually call such a rash, unfounded judgment of a person?

6. If you decided that the box contained something valuable or useless, what prompted your decision? Was it a logical decision or a hunch? What's the difference between a hunch and a prejudice?

7. People are like boxes; they all have different wrappings but we can never be sure what is inside them until they open up. Is it a kind of prejudice to judge a person before you get to know what's inside him? How often do person's wrappings actually indicate what's inside?

8. We don't mind if a person makes a bad judgment so long as he is willing to change his mind when he is proven wrong. What happens when he refuses — or when he can't change his mind? What do you do then?
9. From the exercise we have just done we can see that just about all of us are at least slightly prone to prejudice. Just what is prejudice in your opinion?
10. What would be the opposite of prejudice? How can you develop the habit of "not being prejudiced"?

LISTENING

Definition of Listening

The name of the game today seems to be encounter, communication, honesty, dropping the masks. A lot of talk is devoted to the need for better interpersonal communication, and any teacher who has earned a week's salary has heard at least one student say: "Oh, I just can't communicate with him. He doesn't understand me."

Communication begins, not with speaking, but with listening. There is nothing new in this principle, but when a student feels no one understands him, whether it's his parents, his peers or his teachers, he often thinks the problem can be resolved if the other person would only listen. In fact, the beginning of the solution to his problem is for him to improve his own capacity to listen.

Listening admits of varying degrees. As a vehicle of communication, listening must focus on the other person, not just what the other person is saying. It is listening in such a way that an atmosphere of communication is created; the other person will be able to hear us because he feels we have heard him, that we are "in touch" with *him* and not just with what he is saying. The more we can demonstrate that we hear what the other person is really saying, the more we create an atmosphere where he can afford to hear us.

A good counselor does this for a living. He listens so he can establish contact with the real person and not just the exterior of the person. Once he is in touch he can then share his experience and insights with the counselee and help him understand himself. Of course, a counselor is a professionally trained listener, and must hear things most of us don't need to hear in normal communication with others. But the principle is the same. If communication is to take place, someone must begin it by listening to what the other is saying.

What does a person listen for? What is he trying to hear? Certainly the meaning of the words the other person is saying. But that meaning is shaded and further defined, perhaps even contradicted, by what is not expressed in words: mood, feelings of fear or embarrassment, the overall attitude. Facial expression, tone of voice, even bodily position are part of the total communication of another person. For example. There are probably a thousand different ways to say "hello." Each one would convey something else about the speaker, depending on how he says it and how he looks when he says it.

This capacity to listen is a natural gift for some people. We call it sensitivity. But this ability to listen can be cultivated. Anyone who wants to can develop the capacity. It just requires a conscious alertness which can become a habit in a short time.

Importance of Listening

Adolescents are very preoccupied with the problem of communication and with interpersonal relations. This is especially true in their relations with their parents. It is also true in regard to peer relationships. Many students feel lonely and alienated from their peers and blame it on lack of real communication. This is not just a problem for adolescents, however. Many marriages grow stale because the couple feels there is no communication taking place between them. And in life in general, in the office, in relations between the boss and the worker, in normal social settings, a common complaint is the lack of communication. Therefore, any effort to help students understand better the art of listening and the overall nature of personal communication is bound to have beneficial effects, both immediate and long range.

Problems Related to Listening

The biggest single problem with developing an awareness of the importance of listening as the foundation for communication comes from the psychological make-up of the adolescent. He has a strong need to be understood because he is at the same time struggling to understand himself. He often experiences an urgency in his efforts to communicate and to be understood. For him to first take the time to listen can be very difficult. He wants "his turn" before he has really heard the other person, and is often so eager to express himself that he can't wait until he has established contact with the other person. This is further complicated by the fact that in his dealings with adults such as his parents, he is already convinced from past experience that they either can't or won't really listen to him and understand him.

There is no easy solution to this problem. Urgency and bad experiences from the past can only be countered by times when listening worked and did create a good communication with someone. Which means that the student will have to be encouraged to attempt the "listening approach" as an experiment so that he can experience the effect it has. To simply tell him about it will accomplish little.

A second problem is the burden this topic places on the teacher to be a good listener himself. There is a certain fairness involved. You can't really ask students to practice this type of concerned listening — which sometimes requires heroic generosity on their part — unless they recognize that this is how *you* operate with *them*. My own teaching experiences convince me that students will tolerate failures in a teacher, but they'll never tolerate hypocrisy — and they can smell it out with uncanny accuracy. To put it another way, students won't make the effort to listen to others if they feel you are not making the effort to listen to them. To talk about communication as a value puts the teacher in a "physician, cure thyself" situation — and that can be a problem.

On the positive side, since adolescents are so naturally concerned about communication, the topic generates immediate interest. This interest will be sustained if they begin to *experience* the value of what you are sharing with them.

Cultivating the Capacity to Listen

The exercise we are suggesting has proven effective in demonstrating to students what you mean by listening. That is the first step: demonstrating that listening means more than hearing words. It means hearing the person. Once they understand what you mean by listening and they understand that good listeners create an atmosphere of communication, the next step is to encourage them to experiment on their own. Suggest that they try "listening" to their parents, or to some peer with whom they have difficulty. Not with any special purpose — that would be phony — but just to see if by being a good listener in a given situation they do in fact create an atmosphere of understanding where communication can really take place. This practice of listening can be done anywhere. At the supper table, in the cafeteria, on the bus, between classes.

Once they are more conscious of what you mean by listening, there will be many classroom situations in which you can point out that they aren't "listening to you" or in their mutual discussion they aren't "listening to each other." This serves to keep them aware of the need to listen whenever they are dealing with others. From that point on, it is sufficient to remind them of the importance of listening from time to time and to encourage them to continue to experiment with it. My experience indicates that many students pick up this habit quickly since it is something they have an opportunity to do everyday, almost all day long. And they are also easily convinced that it does help them to communicate with others.

One other point may be helpful. If you have already treated the topics on trust, respect and prejudice in this book, the relation between them and this topic should be obvious. It would be good to remind students of the key ideas they had discussed regarding these topics to help them see the relationships. I have in mind such things as the fact that you won't listen if you don't respect the other person or if you are prone to have a closed mind. In other words, remind them that communication depends on more than listening.

Suggested Exercise for Experiencing Listening
Purpose:
> To involve the students in a listening activity so they can discover for themselves just how well they do listen, and to motivate them to improve.

Preparation:
> The students should be paired off in some random fashion. For best results, however, avoid pairing two close friends together.

Instructions:
1. Explain to the students that they are going to take turns talking to one another for the purpose of discovering how well they can listen. Stress the importance of a serious mood. If the group is giddy, the exercise will have little effect. The rules are these:
   a. Each person is to talk for three minutes about his parents or guardian, telling his partner whatever he thinks is significant about them. After the first person finishes (it is good to announce when three

minutes are up) the second member of the pair begins doing the same thing.

b. When a person is talking, the listener should not speak, interrupt or ask questions. He should simply listen.

c. The conversations should be kept in a low tone so as not to disturb the other pairs and to insure privacy. When they understand what they are to do, have them begin; after three minutes are up, have the speaker become the listener.

2. When both partners have had their turn, explain that now you are going to test how well they listened. Based on what they heard, one person is to tell his partner how he thinks his partner *feels* about his parents. Specifically he should try to pick out what his partner thinks is the *best* thing about his parents, and what *most* upsets him about his parents. When he has done this, the partner judges whether or not he was accurate. Then the second person goes through the same process and his accuracy is judged in turn. Through this part of the exercise the students should get a better feel of what you mean by listening not just to words but to the whole person, his feelings, his attitudes, etc.

3. Now the process is repeated with a new topic. Each partner should take turns talking three minutes about himself, stating what he thinks are the most significant things about himself. When both have had a turn, they are tested for good listening by answering this question to one another: How does your partner feel about himself; what does he think are his best qualities and what does he most dislike about himself?

When this is completed the students should be ready to enter into a general discussion on the topic of listening as a mode of communication that helps people to get to know each other better.

Note: The exercise and subsequent discussion can be rendered more effective by briefing one person ahead of time to give his partner the impression that he is uninterested and distracted and not really listening. When discussion is in progress single out the "slighted" partner for his reactions. It can often illustrate very graphically the effects on communication when someone does not at least try to listen.

Discussion of Listening

1. How did you feel when you were talking? Self-conscious? Did you feel that the other person was really trying to listen to you? Did this make it easier for you to talk?

2. What are some indications that a person is really trying to listen to you? Can you fake an appearance of listening even though you are not?

3. In this kind of situation, which do you prefer — to be the listener or the speaker?

4. How well do you feel your partner zeroed in on what you were feeling and what you were really saying? Was anyone surprised by the way his partner answered the questions about what he was saying and feeling?

5. Do you think it would be good if everyone tried to listen to you as intently as we tried to listen to each other in this exercise? How would it affect your willingness to communicate?

6. If you attempted to listen intently, as we tried to do here, to your parents, do you think it would improve your communication with them? Why? Why not?

7. As a listener, do you feel that you learned some new things about your partner, even though you had talked to him

before, precisely because you really concentrated on listening? Do you think listening is a good way to get to know someone?

8. Is there more to communication than listening? What, for instance?

9. What happens when you simply don't like someone? Can you still listen to him?

10. How much real listening takes place in a situation like the school cafeteria? Does much listening take place in relation to teachers and students? If not, why not?

THE CLASH OF INDIVIDUAL FREEDOMS

Definition of the Clash of Freedoms

In Chapter Four, *Freedom and Responsibility*, we discussed the tug that exists between the use of freedom and the responsibility for that use. In this chapter we are concerned with the conflict between personal freedom and the freedom of others.

The controversy over ROTC on college campuses is a good example of this clash. Some students, exercising their personal freedom, attempt to have ROTC removed from campuses. Whatever the arguments these students may give for their actions, and whatever the arguments given by those who oppose them, the point is that in this kind of conflict one group feels that the only way it can be free is to impose its will on others. It is like saying "The only way I can be free to pursue my convictions is to force these same convictions on others." This obviously takes away the freedom of "the others," but unfortunately it is not always looked at that way.

A more common example often occurs in the "one TV household." Often, a person who exercises his freedom to watch what he wants is encroaching on the freedom of others to watch what they want. In a situation like this there is often nothing more at stake than a question of taste, but the dilemma of individual freedoms is as much present here as it is in the far more serious social conflicts of our day.

There is no easy solution to this problem. In fact, as our society becomes more pluralistic, the problem can only increase. As long as we uphold the right to personal freedom for all, and as long as there are different opinions as to what is good for us, people will clash and someone's freedom will be threatened.

One attempt to alleviate this conflict is the idea of a democracy wherein the majority rules. We can't have four presidents at the same time; only the man who receives majority support will govern, and he must govern even over those who preferred someone else. As long as people feel that they had the freedom to promote and to choose their own president, and as long as the election was fair, they acquiesce in this situation. The fact that some segments of society "lose" can, no doubt, plant the seeds of discontent. But it can also give rise to creative opposition. So the democratic process is one viable way for dealing with this conflict of freedoms.

A second solution to the problem comes in the form of compromise. When an impasse is reached, or when no majority is present to make the decision, the groups involved must be willing to give up their freedom in one area in order to protect it in another. This too is a humane approach, but it is somewhat negative. In a sense, everyone loses. Also some problems, like issues involving deeply personal convictions, matters of conscience, protection of one's family, love for country, etc., simply don't allow compromise. The principles involved seem too crucial to a person's sense of integrity to be sacrificed and he is left with the decision to maintain his position whatever the consequences. This can be a very noble attitude, but mankind has experienced many tragic wars as a result. So compromise, while effective in some areas of human conflict, is not a universal solution.

A third solution, one that seems to work best in small groups, is consensus. Consensus is similar to compromise in that the participants may have to alter their original demands. But there is a key difference. Through openness and discussion the participants are able to discover and enter into the convictions and feelings of each other. They "reason together" and arrive at a decision with which everyone can agree, a decision in which no one loses and which actually binds the persons together in a new unanimity. Not only can the participants live with the decision; they can actively support it. In consensus, the people change their *views* and not just their demands.

While these three solutions are effective in preserving individual freedom despite differences of opinion, it must be remembered that we are dealing with a kind of human dilemma. Until political and social structures can be devised which foster consensus, and until mankind at large has overcome its selfishness and suspicion, conflict in individual freedom will be a part of life.

In working on this topic with students, it seems important that this dilemma be made clear. They tend to be idealistic and have a hard time understanding why people can't come to agreement. This topic intends to demonstrate the problem and make them more aware that it is a part of the human condition. It would be a mistake to give them the impression that there is any perfect solution.

Importance of Understanding the Clash of Freedoms

Most strife in human relations, whether it's a marital problem or a world war, has its roots in the conflict of personal freedoms. We can agree that part of the problem stems from the fact that some persons have unrealistic concepts regarding their own rights. Also some people simply have no regard for the rights of others and have no intention of cooperating with others. In severe cases of this latter, we are dealing with psychopaths, an extreme example of which would be a Hitler or a Stalin.

In daily living, however, the problem does not necessarily imply unrealistic or evil people. It is just a part of life. The more youth can come to appreciate the scope and depth of this problem and recognize it in their own lives, the better will they be able to cope with it realistically, whether through democratic process, compromise or consensus. And if they find that they must take a stand on an issue involving their personal convictions, they will be aware that those who oppose them are not automatically evil or selfish people, but more often are persons who simply hold convictions different from their own. Just granting another person the right to differ from us is a big step in maintaining humane human relations.

Since young people are just beginning to experience personal freedom and are quite self-conscious about protecting it, this problem is not a theoretical one for them. They are experiencing it in relation to their parents, their teachers, their peers, and adult society at large. Any effort to clarify the full nature of the problem will aid them in making a mature emotional adjustment to it, an adjustment which will be valuable the rest of their lives.

Problems Related to the Clash of Individual Freedoms
Since the topic itself is a problem, to speak of problems related to it seems redundant. Therefore, the main point to keep in mind is youth's natural sensitivity regarding personal freedom. It is something new to them, something they still do not possess completely, something they feel they must wrestle from their parents by endless debates or overt rebellion. As a result, they will be naturally suspicious of attempts to qualify that freedom in terms of the rights or freedom of others. You will find the best approach to be one in which you deal with the conflicts in freedom they experience among their peers. This will demonstrate that the problem affects all persons; it is not just a problem that exists in the generation gap.

Another point to remember is that the solution to this problem lies largely in people's ability to communicate, to understand

and respect one another. Youth must become aware of this dimension of the problem. Unless an atmosphere of communication and respect exists between persons, there is no hope of resolving this conflict in wills.

Cultivating an Awareness of the Clash of Freedoms

The first step is to convince students that the conflict of freedom and rights between persons is not something they alone experience. Too often, because of their own personal conflicts with parents, they become convinced that the problem is unique to them. They need to see it as a part of the total human picture. Next it is good to help them get into the habit of seeing things from the other person's point of view. Some of the other topics, such as *Respect* (Chapter Five) and *Listening* (Chapter Eight), can be useful here. The more empathy they can develop for others, the more they will be able to work together to reconcile differences. Role-playing exercises can often be helpful in this regard.

Another step is to demonstrate that the capacity to reason with others and to compromise is a mark of maturity. In their idealism, young people sometimes feel that compromise is a dirty word, a form of "copping out." You will have to illustrate to them all the instances in which they are in fact engaged in compromise — obeying stop signs, agreeing on the proper spelling of a word, following a schedule in school — so that everyone's rights can be protected and people can live and communicate together harmoniously.

The universal nature of the problem, the need for empathy, the necessity of compromise — these are the general principles young people will need to understand. From this point on it is best to deal with specific problems — political, social, familial or school — in which a conflict of freedom and rights is involved. They should be allowed to work through these problems and test the possible solutions: democratic process, compromise, consensus. Even if they can come up with no good solution to a specific problem, an important lesson is learned, namely that quick solutions like violence (a more advanced form of the infantile tantrum), dropping out, or breaking off communication accomplish nothing. They will be learning that some problems have to be lived with, others will be solved only through patience and time, and a few will require heroism and generosity. But at no time is a problem solved when an individual loses his own personal freedom and is forced to accept the will of another.

Suggested Exercise for Experiencing the Clash of Individual Freedoms

Purpose:

> To give the students an experience of the kind of conflict that can result when two people's exercise of their freedom clash with one another.

Preparation:

> You will need no props.
>
> Divide students into pairs, preferably matching boys with boys and girls with girls.
>
> Arrange students in such a way that each person is directly across from his counterpart who is standing on the opposite side of the room.
>
> Students are to fold their arms across their chest.

Instructions:

> 1. Explain that the exercise is a test in each person's strength of will and his convictions regarding personal freedom.
> 2. The object is for each student to walk from one side of the room to the other *in as direct a line as possible.* Make it clear that each person has this right and is free to exercise it. Since the members of each pair, walking

toward each other in a straight line, will meet at some point, one of them will have to either back up or step aside so that the other can continue on to the opposite side of the room. Tell them that the person who does this is indicating weakness of will or lack of concern for his personal freedom.

3. The exercise is to be done in silence. Do not outlaw pushing; however, don't encourage it either. Simply do not make any reference to the possibility of physical force as a means for maintaining a straight path.

4. Once the exercise begins, allow about three minutes for the students to attempt to work out solutions or to test one another. If after that period they begin to laugh and break the seriousness of the mood, it would be time to stop and begin the discussion/reaction.

Discussion of the Clash of Individual Freedoms

1. Did you feel a little threatened in that your strength of will and your sense of freedom were being tested against another person? How did you react to that? Did it make you more determined? Did you try to think of some way to avoid the conflict that seemed inevitable?

2. Did you find that not being able to talk made the problem more difficult to resolve? What do you think you could have done if you were able to talk to the other person?

3. Were there any ways in which both persons' freedom and rights could be equally protected?

4. Even if you did not attempt to use force to gain your right of passage, did you feel tempted to? What prevented you? A dislike of violence? The awareness that the other person was physically stronger than you?

5. (If anyone actually succeeded in forcing another person to step aside or turn back) Did you feel that somehow you still

hadn't proven anything or that in some sense you actually showed less strength of will, or did you feel comfortable with your victory?

6. (If any pair succeeded in arriving at an agreement to both step aside an equal distance so no one actually lost) How did you arrive at this solution? Were you satisfied with it under the circumstances? Do you think this kind of solution is the best?

7. Can you think of other real-life situations where you have been in this kind of direct confrontation with another and where both of you had equal right to your own conviction? How did you resolve it if you did? Did you end up arguing? Did you both go away mad? Did anyone win or lose?

8. Is this kind of conflict common between various groups in society? What ones? How do these groups resolve the problem? What are some of the alternatives?

9. Do you know what consensus is? How does it work? What is required?

10. Can you anticipate that you will find yourself in many real-life conflicts of this nature as you grow older? What in your opinion is the best way to handle them?

MALE-FEMALE

Definition of Male-Female

Unisex, woman's liberation, respectable homosexuality — these are some manifestations in our society of changing attitudes toward the male and female roles. Whether they are passing fads, symptoms of a sick society or truly human developments can be debated. And that is the idea behind this topic. We are not concerned in any direct way with the manifestations we just mentioned. We are interested in an experiential examination of how it feels to be male and female. If this can be clarified for students, if they have some experienced facts to work with, then they are in a position to judge changing sexual trends objectively, to see if these are a step forward or backward in the history of human development.

Note that the topic is not concerned with male vs. female, but with male-female. There is no attempt to prove dominance or weakness in terms of talents, intellectual capacity and the like. Using the biological model of male-female which manifests complementary though distinct roles for human reproduction, we are assuming that the male and female are also complementary in other areas of human life, and that persons have *some* distinct roles precisely because they are male or female. In other areas, being male or female makes no particular difference since either a man or a woman can function equally well. The question is: in what ways are men and women complementary and in what ways are they equal?

This is a most difficult question to answer. The male dominance in our cultural traditions has resulted in some artificial distinctions in roles. Many of these are being shattered today as women prove they can function as well as men in roles like management, politics, science and even mechanics, manual labor and soldiery. Others remain to be challenged. Only history will tell if woman can or should be taken from the protective pedestal that a male-oriented society has reserved for her.

In regard to this question of complementarity rather than competition, Jung has made a significant contribution. He maintains — and verifies by some clinical observation — that each person possesses an "animus" and an "anima." The animus is what we normally consider masculine traits; the anima is what we consider feminine traits. In his approach, Jung sees the male as possessing a conscious animus which allows him to be aggressive, rational, etc., the qualities which we tend to stereotype as "masculine." However, each man possesses an unconscious anima, qualities like sensitivity, gentleness, receptivity — traits we usually consider "feminine." The reverse, of course, is true of women: they possess a conscious anima and an unconscious animus. These unconscious traits need to be released, made conscious and accepted, if a man or woman is to become a complete person.

Our western culture discourages such a development except vicariously. By a man's relationship with a woman, by his support and encouragement of her qualities of gentleness, sensitivity and the like, he lives out his unconscious self through her. (This for Jung is the psychological basis for the man-woman attraction.) The same thing, of course, holds for a woman. She lives out her unconscious male qualities by her identification with a man.

This anima-animus is the psychological basis for the complementary natures of man and woman. While both sexes possess the same qualities, what is conscious in the one is unconscious in the other. The question revolves around the possibility of people realizing their unconscious traits not vicariously but by directly maintaining them as a part of their total personality. For a person becomes whole (puts the two parts together) by accepting both the conscious and unconscious dimensions, so that the unconscious part becomes conscious and is embraced. If this normal complementary relationship is restored, we could perhaps progress to the point where neither man nor woman would feel the need to oppress each other, but could help each other become the male-female person that each of us is.

Psychology continues to study the male-female question in terms of such capacities as imagination, creativity, emotional stability, and specific intellectual talents like math or languages. The results thus far indicate that men and women do differ in how they approach reality and how they react to it, but it is still unclear as to how much these differences are culturally conditioned and how much they are rooted in what can be called a male or female psyche. Nor has psychology proven that men or women are better at certain things; it has only demonstrated that they approach certain things differently.

Importance of Male-Female Understanding
It has been my experience in working with students on such questions as dating, falling in love, physical sex and friendship that little real progress can be made until they grasp the complementary roles of the sexes on more than a physical level. Also, it seems that adolescence is an ideal time for treating the topic of complementary psychologies, since young people are very eager to learn more about themselves as sexual persons and are also very eager to develop personal relationships. Being an adult, male or female, is still such a new experience for them that they are not yet fixed in any defined pattern of self-understanding. In

short they are still very open to learn the meaning of male-female.

The value of introducing this topic to the students, then, lies primarily in its ability to demonstrate for them that there are "psycho" as well as "somatic" differences between men and women, and that these differences are intended to be complementary, not antagonistic. Men and women need each other, not just for providing the two cells out of which new humans develop, but also to be full persons. "Male" and "female" are incomplete ways of being. Unless male and female can inter-relate on the psychological as well as on the physical level, neither will reach fulfillment. Actually, the psychological relationship is more critical than the physical. If this can be demonstrated, the students may acquire the motivation to approach male-female differences positively in order to discover how they can help one another, instead of negatively to determine "who is better."

In the context of complementary psychologies the whole question of marriage is raised above the biological level for the students. The same is true, as I mentioned, regarding their present experience of dating, falling in love, physical sex and friendship. Thus the topic can serve as a good lead-in for a study of those areas. Aside from this perennial reason for broaching the male-female question, the topic has a particular timeliness. Our society is undergoing a kind of "sexual revolution" not just in morals but in the very definition of male-female roles in society. There is so much superficial and popularized commentary concerning sexuality being made on TV talk shows, Sunday supplements and family magazines, that youth can become easily misled into adopting distorted or inaccurate attitudes about themselves and the male-female concept in general. If this topic does nothing more than introduce them into the habit of becoming more critical of these sources of information about sexuality, you are protecting them from some serious misconceptions. On the positive side, since they are at a stage of development in which they are consciously forming judgments about themselves and others as sexual beings, the discovery of the complementary dimension in the male-female psychologies becomes invaluable in forming a healthy self-concept and healthy relationships with others.

Finally, in an age like ours which has become more self-conscious about physical sex and its enjoyment than the Victorians ever dreamed of being — through the effort of trying to free ourselves from Victorian self-consciousness — the topic tends to restore the balance by approaching sexuality as a psychological as well as a biological way of being. It makes it possible to view physical sexuality — including our preoccupation with figures, deodorants and youthfulness — in the larger context of the whole person and wholistic personal relationships. This enables students to gain a more realistic perspective of sexuality than the limited view presented in magazines like *Playboy* or *Cosmopolitan*, both of which typify our over-reactions to the Victorian mores, and makes it possible to de-emphasize our excessive concern about developing beautiful physical attributes.

Problems Related to Male-Female Understanding

You can't open a class by asking "Are boys different than girls?" without expecting a few snickers and under-the-breath comments. Which indicates the first problem related to the topic. Male-female will have all kinds of undertones for most adolescents so it is difficult to approach it in an objective way. It is necessary to avoid giving the impression that you are dealing with sex or sexuality until they realize what you mean by the terms in connection with this topic. It is best to introduce the topic as a study in the psychology of persons — which it is — and as a study in personal relationships. Once this has been explained, it will be easier to talk about male-female or boy-girl relationships without conjuring up the idea of "just another sex talk," and without creating self-consciousness, especially in a mixed class.

A second problem, from my experience, centers on the fact that most students tend to approach the topic as a competition between males and females — due to their cultural background, I suppose, but also due to their own insecurity about their sexuality at this stage in their development. It becomes necessary from the start to introduce the topic in as positive a way as possible, stressing the interdependence of the sexes and their mutual aid to one another.

A third problem will be the difficulty in making concrete the differences in male-female. So many differences, such as a man's ability at math as compared with a woman's ability with language, can be explained largely through cultural conditioning. Even though there are psychic causes for this, the influence of culture and the many "exceptions to the rule" will lead students to question whether all differences beyond the physical are not acquired differences. This of course, goes to the heart of what we are attempting to demonstrate. In cases such as this, I have not always been able to delineate the differences, but at least I have succeeded in raising doubts about the theory that all differences are acquired — which is a good first step for more serious consideration of the whole nature of sexuality. It gets beyond the purely physical and materialistic level.

Cultivating an Understanding of Male-Female

The first step is to raise the question itself and the suggested exercise is intended to do this. Even if this exercise does not demonstrate definitively that there are complementary differences in the male-female, you now have a reason to continue to pursue it.

One of the best ways to do this is through observation, both introspective and in terms of other people. For example, a good experiment for students to undertake is to observe themselves throughout a typical day — the things they do, the decisions they make, their reactions to situations — and keep asking themselves the question: If I were a boy (girl), would I do this differently? Why? Because of cultural training? Or simply because I am a girl (boy)? Often they will discover that they can't really answer the questions, simply because they are not sure how a person of the opposite sex would typically react to a situation. This heightens curiosity about the opposite sex's psychological make-up and convinces them they can't take others for granted. Another useful activity is for them to observe their parents or other married couples, keeping in mind the question: What are the unique psychological contributions each person makes to the other?

One of the best ways to discover in practical terms the different psychologies of the sexes is through friendship. If a boy and girl in a dating situation — or a brother and sister of comparable age — simply talk about how they approach things such as their likes and dislikes, their fears and joys, what they are looking for in life, etc., they will discover many differences in approach even though they may be very similar in basic values. In this kind of relationship, especially in a dating relationship, it becomes rather clear that the male-female psychologies complement each other in a variety of ways. All that is required is that the young people consciously seek to discover these ways.

Once the students are aware of the question and actively seek to determine which (if) male-female differences other than the biological exist, a side benefit results in that they usually become much more sensitive to each other and respectful of the uniqueness of the other. This is a much healthier attitude for forming friendship and preparing for marriage than the narrow mentality that stays with superficial personality traits, appearance and physical sexuality. Dating ceases to be a subtle form of combat in which each person is attempting to dominate the other (an apt description of dating in our society) and becomes an exciting mutual discovery of interdependence and cooperation which can become the foundation for a lasting relationship.

Suggested Exercise for Experiencing Male-Female Understanding
Purpose:

> To create a situation in which boys and girls can discover the different though complementary aspects of the masculine and feminine psychology.

Preparation:

> Pair students off into boy-girl sets in some random fashion.
> Pencil and paper for each student.

> Note: The exercise is effective only in co-educational classes. If you have an uneven number of boys and girls, match two boys with a girl or two girls with a boy, to handle the extra boys or girls.

Instructions:

1. Each student is asked to draw a list of the ten most important things he or she would look for in buying a house.

2. After the lists are completed, the students are to form into their couples (or groups):
   a. to compare their lists, noting similarities and differences,
   b. to synthesize the two lists so they end up with one list of the ten most important features to look for in a house.

   In order to do the synthesizing they will have to compromise with one another and discuss together the relative advantages of their different ideas so they can decide on which points to keep in the final list.

   Allow sufficient time for this since it is the most educational part of the experience.

3. When the lists are complete, allow time for the students

to compare their finished list with those of the other pairs. This should heighten interest. When they have had time for this, you may call them all together for a general discussion.

Discussion of Male-Female

1. Do you feel your final list was better or worse than the one you drew up alone? Why? Why not?
2. Did you have a hard time agreeing on what should be included and what should be left out of the final list? How did you arrive at your conclusions?
3. Were you able to work together or did you find yourselves competing in making your decisions? Did anyone "win" or dominate?
4. Were you surprised to find how much the list you drew up differed/agreed with the ones others drew up? How do you account for the similarities? The differences?
5. Insofar as the individual lists differed, do you think this was based on being a boy or a girl or was there some other reason? Do you think girls are simply conditioned to think differently than boys or is there a real psychological difference between boys and girls?
6. Were you nervous or did you feel embarrassed or threatened during the exercise? Why?
7. Did you feel you could really communicate and understand the other person's approach? Did you feel the other person was able to understand yours?
8. This exercise was primarily an example. Do you think that men and women generally see and approach things differently? Do you think a combined effort in which men and women worked together on projects, etc. would be more successful than a project in which they worked alone or even competed?

9. Do you see any implications, based on this discussion, regarding dating and marriage and how men and women should relate to one another?
10. How important do you feel it is to understand how the opposite sex approaches reality? How could you go about getting a better understanding of the opposite sex?

GENERATION GAP

Definition of the Generation Gap

There are actually several kinds of generation gaps. First there is the perennial gap that occurs as the adolescent withdraws from his parents and begins to test out his own personhood. This we can best term a *developmental gap*, since it is both healthy and necessary if the child is to become mature and self-directed. Painful as it is to parent and adolescent alike, it is traditionally resolved in a matter of a few years when the child is clearly a young adult and is capable of entering into an adult relationship with his parents.

There is a second kind of gap, common but avoidable, that often occurs simultaneously with the developmental gap. We might call it an *empathy gap*. It is caused by the fact that adolescent and parent are unable to empathize with each other due to circumstantial differences. For example, the young girl who has fallen in love for the first time and who hopes to find empathy in her new enthusiasm for life, encounters a mother who is experiencing menopause. Physically distraught and emotionally drained, the mother is not in a very good condition to enter into her daughter's excitement. Another example is the son who is keyed up about getting his own car but confronts a father preoccupied with financial problems. For the father, the son's enthusiasm is seen simply as an additional drain on the money. In both instances the young person goes away feeling like a victim of the generation gap. This empathy gap can be overcome if circumstances change or if it is recognized for what it is. However, it can become the cause of a deeper gap if it persists over a long period of time.

In addition to a developmental gap and an empathy gap, there is a third kind, a *values gap*. This kind of gap is not restricted to adolescents and parents. It can occur between people the same age, a husband and wife for instance, or a brother and a sister.

The cause of this values gap is sociological and psychological. Persons approach reality differently and they are to a large degree conditioned to accept certain values because of their cultural experience. Hence, a farmer and an account executive from Chicago, though both the same age, are likely to experience this kind of gap in values. The same is true of the black and white man, the southerner and northerner, the middle class and the poor, the blue collar worker and the white collar worker. It has happened in our time that this kind of values gap has also occurred between many of the high school and college students and the "over thirty" set. The causes are complex, but basically what has happened is that the young people feel separated from parents and other adults, not only in the normal, even desired developmental sense and in the circumstantial sense of lack of empathy, but also in the sense that they have rejected the basic values of the culture which conditioned their parents and other adults.

This values gap is dangerous enough when it occurs between two adult segments of society. It can be devastating when it occurs between youth and adults who are already separated in the developmental and empathetic sense. While adult groups thus separated can disagree with each other in socially acceptable ways such as the voting poll or the law court, adolescents do not have this kind of recourse. They are left with three basic options: dropping out, taking to the streets, or waiting. Dropping out can mean anything from running away from home and taking drugs, to losing oneself in the more harmless frivolities of their peer culture. Taking to the streets can include senseless vandalism (breaking school windows on a lark) or organized, political revolution. Waiting is the least appealing of the three options. It is often labeled a "cop out."

It should be noted that we can't blame these negative reactions, either dropping out or violence, on youthful impetuosity or lack of responsibility. When a whole society seems opposed to your values and when that society has not provided you with an effective means of challenging it — we must admit peaceful demonstrations have not proven very effective — then frustration is bound to mount. Frustration can result in irrational actions but the cause of frustration is not necessarily irrational.

The best solution to the developmental gap is time. It takes time for the adolescent to feel secure in his autonomy. The process can be hastened or held back by parents who either encourage or discourage this development, but time ultimately resolves the problem.

The best solution for the empathy gap is communication, *two-way* communication. If the student and the parent can pinpoint the areas where they are failing to understand one another, these can be worked out together. Where this kind of communication is impossible, little can be done until the circumstances causing the problem change.

With the values gap, we face something of a dilemma similar to the one described in Chapter Nine, *The Clash of Individual Freedoms*. The difficulty is that young people do not have equal opportunity with adults in making the decisions that foster or discourage certain values of our society. So solutions like compromise, democratic process and consensus cannot be employed.

107

Protest, violent or peaceful, may relieve frustration but has had little effect on altering society's values. Often it only broadens the gap that exists.

There is no solution for the values gap that can be effected in the classroom (for example, you will not be able to lower the voting age to allow students to immediately participate in society's decisions). The most realistic thing that can be accomplished is to bring students to an awareness of the full nature of the dilemma so that they can distinguish the generation gaps of development and empathy from the more critical gap of values. The suggested exercise is intended to do this.

Importance of the Generation Gap

The generation gap has become a kind of popularized myth surrounded by all kinds of misconceptions and pseudo-solutions. As a result, the various specific gaps are misunderstood. For that reason, it seems important that we help students to get a full understanding of the nature of the several "gaps" involved so they can deal with each one intelligently.

Society is split into an under-thirty and an over-thirty group, each at odds with the other and threatening to develop into a permanent two-society situation. This would be disastrous, especially since it could be avoided if the nature and causes of the split were better understood. That is the real reason why it is important that we help students clarify what is taking place.

As mentioned above, there are no immediate solutions to the values gap, and this gap is deepened when the more traditional gaps between generations are allowed to complicate the situation, or are treated as if they were all the same problem. If a teacher can help students realize this, even if he can't give them immediate solutions, he is at least creating a mentality in which solutions can be worked out in humane ways. That is the real purpose of treating this topic.

Problems Related to the Generation Gap
The biggest problem I have faced in connection with this topic is
the fact that some students have "given up" on adults, despaired
of ever being able to communicate with them. Since young people generally do not realize that the developmental and empathy
gaps will in fact decrease as they grow older, they feel there is no
hope of ever resolving the deeper and more serious gap of values.
To this is added the frustration they have experienced, heighten-
ed by their natural impatience, when they tried to sincerely communicate with adults and effect changes in society, whether local
changes in their school situation or national changes like foreign
policy.

Another problem to anticipate is the amount of emotion that
is related to the topic, making it difficult to deal with it objectively. For just about every student, the generation gap in one form
or another has been experienced very keenly. It may have been a
recent argument with their parents over the deadline for getting
home — during which they made no headway in making their
own position understood or accepted. It may have been a recent
experience of apparent indifference on the part of their parents.
It may have been a serious debate with them over church at-
tendance. Regardless of the form the gap took, the experience is
usually fresh enough that students tend to view the whole
question in the light of their most recent experience and are
unable to rise above their emotions so they can see things
objectively.

Finally, you yourself will sometimes be viewed as the
"enemy" which makes it difficult for you to obtain a hearing.
None of these problems is insurmountable but it is good to be
aware that they are often present when this topic is introduced.

Cultivating an Awareness of the Generation Gap
You will usually have no difficulty in creating interest in the

109

topic in general. The task is to introduce the idea that there are actually several different kinds of gaps. Once this becomes clear, the next step is to deal with various concrete problems — ideally ones the students themselves bring up — by asking the question, "Which kind of gap are we actually dealing with in this instance?" After that has been decided, it is possible to search for a solution to that particular problem. The advantage of this approach is that it gets the whole matter out of the realm of theory and generalization and makes it possible to deal realistically with specific problems. The pragmatism of this approach and the individual success that students experience in dealing with a specific problem reassure them that there is still hope that the generations can ultimately get together.

In the area of the values gaps, even though no immediate solution can be discovered, it at least becomes clear to students what their options are. They can then judge more calmly the comparative advantages of such actions as dropping out or violence against the more constructive, though less immediate, solutions. If you succeed in removing the problem from the realm of blind emotions, mob mentalities and simplistic one-sided solutions, you have taken a big step toward the ultimate solution to the values gap which still lies somewhere in the future of society.

Suggested Exercise for Experiencing the Generation Gap
Purpose:
> To illustrate the nature of the gap and stimulate a more constructive attitude toward it.

Preparation:
> No props are necessary.
>
> Divide students into three groups. Have each group appoint a spokesman to represent it.
>
> If you have a blackboard, put three columns on it with the following headings: grade school, high school, adult.

110

Instructions:

1. Designate one group as "grade school children" (around sixth grade level), designate another as the "high school" group, and the third as the "adult" group.

· 2. Explain that you are going to ask several different questions. Each group is to discuss among themselves and decide upon an answer to the question, based on what they think would be a *typical* answer from the age group they represent. When they have their answer the spokesman is to announce it and you can place it on the board under the appropriate heading.

3. The questions you are to ask are these (or similar ones you develop):

   a. What is the main reason your age group wants money?

   b. What is the importance of a car (a bike for grade schoolers) to your age group?

   c. What kind of music does your age group like?

   d. What kind of TV show or movie would be the favorite for your age group?

   e. What magazine would your age group most likely buy at the drug store?

   f. Of what use is a wristwatch to your age group?

   After you have asked each question and the groups have decided each answer, you can begin the discussion.

   Note: Usually there can be quite a bit of discussion in each group over the "typical" answers to the question. There is no need to rush this.

Discussion of the Generation Gap

1. Now that you can see all the answers of all the groups, comment on any of those similarities or differences that are a surprise to you or with which you would like to agree.

2. Do you think age is the only reason for the differences that do exist in the answers? Did you find much disagreement within your own group over the typical answer? Why?
3. Do you think there really are any "typical" answers from the different age groups to these questions? Or do you think we tend to stereotype each group when in fact the persons in that age group may vary widely in interests, tastes, values?
4. Do you think there is real gap between the age groups? Would you call it a generation gap?
5. Is there anything in the kinds of answers each age group gave that makes the gap insurmountable? For example, is the gap between high school students and adults over music such that there is no room or hope for common interests?
6. Is the difference in tastes between various age groups the real cause for the apparent difficulty they have in communicating? What would be some other obstacles to communication between the age groups?
7. Do you think younger children experience the generation gap that exists between them and high school students in the same way that high school students experience the gap between themselves and adults? What would make it different?
8. Are high school students concerned about the gap that exists between them and grade school students? Should they be? Do they do anything to overcome it? Should they? Is there a parallel relationship between this and the adults' attitude toward adolescents?
9. What eventually eliminates the gap you may now experience between yourself and younger brothers and sisters? Is there any hope the same kind of thing can take place between adolescents and adults?
10. Are there really several kinds of generation gaps caused by several kinds of different things? Can you describe some of these?

HAWK AND DOVE

Definition of Hawk and Dove

As such the labels "hawk" or "dove" are useful only in terms of a person's external position regarding war in general or the political aptness of a particular war. Thus those who support military action are called hawks; those who oppose it, doves. But these labels do not indicate what is within a person; for example, a supporter of a particular war may not by personality be warlike, whereas a person opposing war in general may himself have a very warlike disposition. The point is, peace and war begin within the individual person. The external attitudes are the result of certain cultural conditionings or political convictions. The warlike or peaceable disposition comes from much deeper.

The purpose of the topic is to illustrate this fact to the students, many of whom are doves — perhaps because it is the "in" thing for their peer culture. This in no way means they are insincere about their concern for peace. It simply means that displaying a peace symbol is no real measure of the inner disposition and capacity to act peaceably in trying circumstances. It is important for students to gain some insight into their *inner* disposition toward peace or violence so they can foster the former or correct the latter.

Only a mentally sick person regards war or violence as a good in itself. Even the most ardent hawk in the political sense ordinarily regrets what he considers the necessary side effects (death and destruction) of war as a means of preserving a country's rights. So it is not a question of some persons favoring peace and others favoring war. It is a question of how someone instinctively reacts when confronted with a threat to his person or to the person of his loved ones. The warlike reaction is what must be confronted and rooted out if we are ever to have real peace both in our interpersonal relationships and in our international politics.

A warlike disposition can be discovered in confrontations between the races, in confrontations between parents and children, in confrontations between peers. That this warlike disposition seems to infect most of us more than we'd like to admit can be observed in something as apparently harmless as football cheers during a high school game or in our instinctive hope that the "good guy" will clobber the "bad guy" who has been taking advantage of our hero for the first hour of a movie. We grant, as do reputable psychologists, that some of the spectator violence in our society is a healthy vicarious outlet for the instinctive violence that seems to be part of the heredity of the human animal. But it also serves to indicate just how much of this instinct we still have under the surface of our more civilized demeanor.

Even when our civilized veneer inhibits us from actually becoming physically violent, emotional hostility can find many subtle ways to attack the "enemy." Sarcasm, ridicule, the silent treatment, the freeze-out are just a few of the ways we go to war with others. And if these strategies are subtle enough they can actually do more harm than physical violence, which is easily recognized and thus provides some opportunity for self-defense. Divorce counseling clinics, for example, are filled with fighters who have been sparring for years in these psychological wars and often display the emotional scars to prove it. A little overt hostility, which could have been easily recognized by both partners so they could focus on the causes, would have made it possible to avoid the years of cold war which eventually destroy the marriage.

All of us have these tendencies to use physical or psychological violence as a means for solving differences with others. Some succeed in rooting them out entirely. These are the authentic peacemakers or doves. Others manage to keep the physical violence under control, having learned that this is messy and seldom solves the problem. Yet these same persons are still quite capable of psychological violence and often engage in it without being aware of it. Regardless of their political position on war, both hawks and doves in this category are in fact still warlike. Finally a few are in the habit of using physical violence as an acceptable way to resolve their conflicts. These we regard as immature if not criminal.

Students need to be aided in discovering not only the degree of their tendency toward violence, but also the way they handle hostility when they do not use physical violence. By the time we reach our teens, most of us have perfected various ways of punishing others without reverting to violence. Unless we become conscious of these battle tactics we will use them consistently — on friends, at work, in marriage, with children. As a result, we are fostering war, often engaged in war, despite our very peaceful external actions. In pragmatic terms, these unnoticed ways of attacking others become the cause for the disintegration of relationships. These same tendencies, when viewed on a national level, make it possible for international wars to be not just tolerated, but even encouraged. And because this foundation for war is subconscious, even political doves may share in the responsibility for a war without realizing it.

Importance of Understanding Hawk and Dove

The importance of this topic is accentuated by the physical conflicts taking place around the world and the deep divisions within the country. There is critical value in any attempt to foster peace during these times. However, our concern here is not directly with international affairs. It is with developing in the student a greater capacity for peaceful relationships in his daily life. Of course, if enough people over a long enough period of time develop this capacity, we would in fact have world peace, but such a long-range goal is a little too large for the scope of one exercise.

Another aspect of our culture makes this topic vital. That is our concern with violence of all kinds — in the streets, on the campuses, between the races, between the generations. Psychologists are still searching for the causes of these phenomena in America so something can be done on a national level to correct them. In the meantime, whatever an individual teacher can do that will aid his students in becoming more conscious of their own potential for violence and for peace will be a valuable step forward. That is the real value of this lesson.

Problems Related to Hawk and Dove

Whenever this topic comes up with students, the most common problem is their doctrinaire, theoretical approach to it. This is especially true of high school students who are our immediate concern. Politically they tend to be pro-peace or doves, not so much because they are always that well informed politically, but because it is part of their overall rejection of the adult establishment, an establishment which in their eyes is pro-war. Thus you could get entangled in a political debate or with theoretical discussions about the beauties of peace which have little direct effect on the actual behavior of the students in terms of their relations with others.

This makes it necessary for you to zero in as quickly as possible on the students' own inner tendencies toward violence or peace. It becomes more important if for political reasons you do happen to favor a military action in a particular case, regardless of your overall concern for peace. For you to introduce the topic of peace would appear phony to them if you did not make it clear that you are talking about a psychological, not a political concept.

A second problem will be the natural defensiveness that is connected with this kind of topic. Everyone likes to consider himself peaceful, even though a degree of violence lurks within all of us. If the impression is given that you are accusing the students of not being peaceful, they will become very guarded — if not hostile. So it is necessary to present the topic in as positive a way as possible. The question is: "How *peaceful* are you?" not "How *warlike* are you?"

Cultivating an Awareness of Hawk and Dove
The first step, as indicated above, is to get students to focus on themselves instead of on the broad political or philosophical question. The next step is to introduce to them the whole idea of psychological hostility, as opposed to physical violence, and the many forms it takes in personal relationships. From there you might ask them to recall as many instances of this kind of hostility as they can, from examples in films and literature and from their own experiences with others. The final step is to encourage them to become more conscious of their own feelings and their own reactions to others in conflict situations. Once they recognize that some of these reactions are in fact hostile ones, despite their general dedication to the ideal of peace, the rest is up to them. You aren't in a position to force upon them changes in personal behavior, but through this approach you can at least lead them to the point where they are aware that some changes

117

are called for. Only they can decide to make the changes in their behavior patterns.

Suggested Exercise for Experiencing Hawk and Dove

Purpose:

> To create a situation in which students will feel within themselves the tendency or pull toward violent means to achieve their goal.

Preparation:

> several packages of penny balloons
>
> a package of straight pins
>
> a ball of string
>
> masking tape

Instructions:

1. Divide students into groups of six to eight. If you are dealing with only one group, divide it in half. Give each group about 12 balloons of *one* color, making sure that each group starts with the same number and that each group has a distinct color. Also give each group some string, some of the pins and some masking tape.

2. Explain the purpose of the activity as follows:

   a. Each group is to assign two balloon men who are to blow up the group's balloons, tie strings to them, and with the masking tape attach their balloons to a portion of a wall you designate as the "target area" (all groups have the same target area).

   b. A time limit should be established of about five to ten minutes for the task.

   c. The group that is able to blow up and attach the most balloons to the target area within the time limit will be judged as having the most teamwork and the most ability to adjust to difficult circumstances.

d. Those members of a group who are not blowing up the balloons are given pins. The pins may be used as weapons to pop the balloons of other groups if they judge that such action will insure their own group ending up with the most balloons in the target area.

Note: Do not indicate that they should pop the balloons of the other groups. Only indicate that the pins might be used for that purpose.

e. After everyone understands the instructions, give each group a few minutes to assign their balloon men and their pin men and to discuss their strategy for protecting their balloons from the pins of another group. Tell them that during the exercise they are not allowed to talk with anyone except the members of their own group. Then begin the exercise.

Note: At no time should you suggest that the object is to destroy the balloons of another group. The object given by you is to place balloons in a designated area. Only by inference do you indicate that *one* way to win is to destroy the balloons of other groups.

f. When the time limit is up, count the balloons in the target area and determine a "winner" — if any balloons are left. Then gather the students for a reaction to the exercise.

Note: If no one attempted to pop the balloons of other groups — which seldom happens — you would want to direct your discussion to that fact and search out how they achieved such a peaceful approach to the task.

Discussion of Hawk and Dove

1. (for the balloon men) How did you feel about your part in the exercise? Did you feel unsafe because you had no pin?

Helpless to defend yourself? If those of another group attacked your balloons, what kinds of reactions did you feel?

2. (for the pin men) What was your first reaction to the exercise? Having a pin, did you immediately decide to pop the others' balloons? Did you expect that other groups would naturally attempt to pop the balloons of your group?

3. If your group was attacked by others while you had no intention of attacking them, what effect did this have on you? Did you want to strike back? Did you feel that now you had to strike back in order to insure your chance to win?

4. Did it occur to you that the whole exercise could have been conducted without popping the balloons of others? That it could have just been a simple race of blowing up balloons and taping them to the target area? Do you recall that I avoided any indication that the object of the exercise was to pop the others' balloons? Where did that idea come from? Why did it start? How come we tend to think in terms of destroying the others' balloons in order to win?

5. How do you think the exercise would have differed if you were not given pins? Did the very idea of weapons create a tendency toward violence?

6. What would have happened if every group was able to get all its balloons in the target area within the time limit? Would there be something wrong with everyone winning?

7. Do you think the fact that you were not allowed to talk with the other groups made it more likely that you would attack each other? What role could communication have played in keeping peace?

8. Once the balloon popping began, did it tend to snowball? If it did, why? Even though no one said the object was to pop balloons, did this in fact become the object? Did it only take one person to begin, to get others started attacking? Why?

9. Did you ever feel you could really trust the other groups to leave your balloons alone? Why or why not?

10. To what degree do you think this exercise symbolizes certain problems in maintaining peaceful human relationships?